I0081599

CODE V. CODE

THE STREET CODE VERSUS THE LEGAL CODE: RETHINKING YOUR BUSINESS TRANSACTIONS

Intellectual Property, Right to Privacy and Contracts
The Empowerment Guide For Athletes, Entertainers
and Entrepreneurs

ELLAKISHA O'KELLEY

CODE V. CODE: THE STREET CODE VERSUS THE LEGAL CODE – RETHINKING YOUR BUSINESS TRANSACTIONS.

Copyright © 2020 by Ellakisha O'Kelley.

All rights reserved. Printed in the United States of America. No part of this book may be used or reproduced in any manner whatsoever without written permission except for quotations and reviews.

Paperback ISBN: 978-1-7354983-0-0
eBook ISBN: 978-1-7354983-1-7

CONTENTS

ACKNOWLEDGMENTS

I am full of gratitude for so much that has gone behind starting and finishing this book. I am thankful first and foremost for the Devine Insight and Universal Presence that I call God, for this project to even be a reality. Thank you, Leanne Gould, for being my personal editor in chief and extending your time as a labor of love. Thank you to all the individuals that contributed to my experiences as a professional athlete—the good, bad, and ugly. Thanks to all my clients that influenced my message in ways that you don't even know. Thank you to my legal interns Emil Tomosunas and Nicholas Pope for tackling the case assignments in a timely manner.

A huge thanks to my mom, Vonda Williamson, who always encourages me and supports all that I do and was just as excited as I was to start and finish this book. Thanks to my Father Anthony Johnson for the words of encouragement. Thank you to my sisters Latisha Williamson and Tranichsha Frazier, who I bounce everything off of and who keeps me true to myself in all my endeavors and made sure I did so in this book. To my niece Zysharia, and nephews Tysio, Qualil, Quilan, and Wriley who motivates me to do my part so that you can share your genius and beauty prosperously with the world. To my daughter and son, Rhiana and Keshaun, I'm giving a huge thank you for your patience and sacrifice. I spent countless hours and days finishing this book, and you all adapted. Love and hugs to my beautiful G-baby, Lila Marie, who inspires me to fight for the future generations. To Tony O'Kelley, thank you for your motivation and willingness to assist in the introduction of my book to the world.

Lastly, I am thankful that Covid-19 created the necessity to quarantine for months where I was able to complete something that I have pushed off for so long.

INTRODUCTION

"Every day, you have the power to choose."
-Michelle Obama

Code v. Code is an empowerment guide that addresses the long-standing battle between the "Street Code" and the "Legal Code" in business transactions involving copyrights, trademarks, rights to privacy, and contracts in the sports, entertainment, and entrepreneurial spaces. Street Code is learned behavior through cultural conditioning or industry behavior that influences the creation of "acceptable" social contracts between parties involved in a business dealing. These social contracts may or may not be upheld in a court of law. Legal Code is a combination of laws established through legislation (statutory) or common law (case law), which may be enforced upon all parties involved in a business dealing should a dispute arise.

The intention behind writing this empowerment guide is to illuminate the path leading to a transformation in how the athlete, entertainer, and entrepreneur experience and handle business relationships and decision-making. This guide will share information that highlights practices and policies – principles and rules – that have worked for and against the owners of the intellectual property they seek to protect. In the highlighted industries specifically, the problems remain the same, only the players change.

This guide discusses the personal and financial effects of operating under the Street Code or Legal Code in each of the four areas mentioned above -- copyright, trademark, right to privacy, and contracts. Knowledge of the differences between the Street Code and the Legal Code will hopefully lead you to an understanding of how to manage your intellectual property effectively now and into the future. "Making it" is more than using your gifts. "Making it" is applying your intelligence and knowledge of the "rules of the game" to get leverage and the ability to define your future.

This empowerment guide delivers a broad discussion on the related topics. The information expressed only touches the surface of the issues and consequences that could be realized. However, the knowledge shared should be enough to spark a fire in individuals that could ignite a flame for change that is far-reaching. The first step in shifting the dynamics of sustainability and ownership in these industries for athletes, entertainers, and entrepreneurs, is to seek heightened awareness and accountability for your actions. This guide does not provide legal advice but is meant to encourage you to be a better advocate for yourself and do a better job of managing your most valuable assets – your creative and athletic talents. As each state has a slightly different Legal Code, the laws that apply to your specific situation may vary. Therefore, hiring an attorney to advise you regarding the issues raised in this guide would be a great option to consider.

As mentioned, this guide is separated into four subjects: copyright, trademark, right to privacy, and contracts and is presented in a legal brief format. You can read the guide straight through or focus on a specific part at any time, in no particular order. Each subject has six sections: Facts, History, Issues, Rules, Application, and Conclusion. **Facts** introduce general information about the subject and why the discussion is essential. **History** provides background information and gives context to the rest of the discussion. **Issues** touch on general questions typically asked, or at least that should be asked regarding the subject. **Rules** explain the applicable Street Code and Legal Code. **Application** shares real-life cases and outcomes to illustrate competing community practices and legal principles. **Conclusion** ties the points made in each section together. These sections may include information that is repetitive. It was done to emphasize the points that would be of great benefit to you to understand fully.

CODE V. CODE

COPYRIGHT

Street Code v. Legal Code

United States (2020)

FACTS

"Any fool can know. The point is to understand."
- **Albert Einstein**

Permission or Forgiveness

Copyright protection is grounded in the U.S. Constitution and is granted by federal law. Copyright law protects original works of authorship that are expressed in a tangible medium such as a writing, recording, or photograph which everyone can see, hear, or touch. Under copyright law, these expressions of original work fixed in a permanent form are considered the property of the author.

Copyright law provides many protections for creatives in the entertainment industry, including protections for songwriting, theatre, and other areas of performing arts, including photographs. There are exceptions to what copyright law protects, even when expressed in a tangible form. Some of the things that are not protected include, but are not limited to, ideas, procedures, methods, concepts, principles, discoveries, titles, names, and slogans.

The entertainment industry faces the most backlash for copyright infringement cases because of the widespread unauthorized use of music, literature, and scripts. Most of the infringement cases in the business and sports industry arise from violations regarding unauthorized use of photographs on social media, marketing, or use on merchandise.

It may be impossible to eradicate the issues of ongoing copyright infringement in these industries. But we can reduce the number of violations done by, or to, an individual by learning and respecting the laws applicable to protecting the rights of original work. Unfortunately, history has shown that we prefer to ask for forgiveness instead of permission. But what if that forgiveness comes with a hefty price tag? Case after case, people are penalized for the illegal use of a copyrighted work. Yet, these penalties don't deter others from doing the same thing. Quite often, we read news reports about celebrities crossing boundaries. Although a celebrity may not have to be as concerned with using someone else's work as if it were his or her own because of their financial status, if an up and coming entertainer replicates this behavior, they may risk forfeiting all the time, energy and effort they put into their work. A major star may have deep pockets or profits from a hit song to mitigate the damage. But if you are not a major star, you may not have deep pockets to pay for forgiveness.

I always tell people that if you have a question about whether it is ok to use someone's work without their permission, as a creator, put yourself in their position. If someone used your work, your unique and creative thoughts, expressions, or images, without permission or acknowledgment, would it be ok? Would you feel disrespected and upset if someone else received credit for your work that you put so much of your time and talent into creating? On top of all of that, would you be upset if they made money from it and you didn't receive a dime? If this is your career, your passion, you want to protect yourself from being disrespected just as much as you should not be the one disrespecting others.

Copyright infringement may affect your career, sometimes before it even gets started, especially if you are one of those individuals who don't take full precautions to protect their work. If you share your ideas before documenting them in a writing, recording, or another tangible medium, you put yourself at risk of someone claiming ownership of your creation. Even if your work is captured in a tangible form, such as a script, logo, or photograph, you may still put yourself in a position of losing your rights if you lack the full understanding of how registering your copyright can provide full protection for you to enforce.

These incidences happen too often with new or independent artists and start-up companies. The typical Street Code mindset of new artists and start-up business owners is that the immediate focus should be on realizing the dream first while gaining an understanding of how the legalities of business side work can come later. Unfortunately, it can be very costly and stressful to deal with copyright issues. Not handling your legal business first is what turns dreams into nightmares. The negative impact of copyright infringement can – and usually does – hurt both the person wronged and the person who is the wrongdoer.

HISTORY

"I did then what I knew how to do.
Now that I know better, I do better."
- Maya Angelou

Practiced Behavior

Music creation and photography are two areas in which copyright infringement frequently occurs. Most of the time, copyright infringement issues arise as a result of historically acceptable practiced behavior. Often, people say, "that's how it has always been done." This is a common explanation to justify unacceptable, and often illegal, decisions to use copyrighted works of others. This behavior created a Street Code that has produced the same outcome over and over again – trouble!

The following sections discuss some of the industry practices born out of the Street Code that influenced the illegal use of original works of music and photography.

Music – Infringement of Musical Works

In the music industry, there is a widespread practice of using an original sound recording and combining it with a new sound recording to create new work. This practice is called sampling. When sampling was made prevalent, it was done so without the permission of the owner of the sampled work. The evolution of sampling is an example of how the Street Code established an "acceptable" practice of using the original work of others without seeking permission. Sampling became an issue when record labels deemed it problematic for the artists of the new work to benefit financially and not share in the profit. As a result, a battle developed between the Legal Code and the Street Code as the artists of the sampled work demanded compensation for its use. These legal battles did not stop artists from unauthorized sampling. The Street Code affects how artists made music then and continues to influence how it is made now.

The music genre that is most known for birthing the art of sampling is hip-hop. During the '60s, '70s, and early '80s, before sampling became an "official thing," partygoers and disc jockeys (DJs) played single or multiple songs by various artists at social gatherings. The artists did not get paid for the performance of their songs at these parties like they can now. DJs just purchased a record, album, or cassette tape and played it for the partygoers. When sampling was born, there was a shift in how DJs played music when they hosted parties. DJs used the music more creatively by manipulating the sound recordings by playing more than one artist's album at the same time to create new "mixes" of music.

The hip-hop culture recognizes DJ Kool Herc as one of the originators cultivating this shift. He would play albums at his parties that he purchased, or otherwise gained possession of, and put his spin on the songs by looping portions of both sound recordings and verses to create a unique repeat. He also used his skill to create a "break." Meaning he would take out the song's full sound, which included the music and singing, to play the break. Other DJs soon used their skills to create or master new sounds by using the same methods.

This form of manipulation inspired a push in musical creativity. DJs went from synchronizing sounds with albums to creating a whole new piece altogether. The DJs accomplished this by playing two albums simultaneously and mixing the beats of both albums. This skill took on many forms DJ to DJ, and the idea of sampling continued to evolve as a result of this masterful experimentation.

DJ Grand Master Flash is the first DJ who used lyricists to rap over the mixes he created at these parties. Gradually, other DJs started adding lyricists or Masters of Ceremony (MC) to entertain alongside them as well. The DJs would use sampling techniques to create beats, and the MC would perform spoken words or "rap" over the beats. This evolution took place in the "underground" community and had not yet hit mainstream music outlets. Eventually, these creative works started to circulate in the community. A DJ named Caz had a group named Cold Crush. DJ Caz's group was the first to record their work on tape while rapping over other artists' sound recordings. This stylistic approach to music creation that was once heard only underground at parties began to grow into something much more.

The Sugar Hill Gang, founded by Sylvia Robinson, took rap from local communities to the airwaves. In 1979, their song, *Rapper's Delight*, was a breakthrough in expanding the hip-hop culture to national platforms of radio and television. The national attention of their song birthed an industry within an industry. More rappers followed this path and began to fill the airways.

Afrika Bambaataa was one of these rappers. He was the leader of a group called Zulu Nation in Brooklyn, New York, and a well-known DJ and MC. Bambaataa recorded a song called *Planet Rock* that sampled a few other artists' recordings. A musical style that was played underground and on tapes was now being heard on a grander scale. With his work reaching the ears of a larger audience, a message was sent that there were no boundaries when creating a hip-hop record. From there on out, the Street Code said it was ok – if not necessary to be a hit – for a hip-hop artist to sample from other artists' creative work.

The success of hip-hop may have made it desirable to sample from other artists' work, but over the years, artists from different genres joined the act. In 2019, the pop singer Katie Perry lost a legal battle against a Christian rapper named Marcus Gray, p.k.a. Flame. A federal jury found her liable for sampling elements of his copyright-protected song, *Joyful Noise,* for her song *Dark Horse.* The jury slapped a $2.8 million verdict on her sending the message that you don't have a right to copy someone else's creative work if you don't get permission from the rightful owner of that copyright. Katie had the verdict overturned on appeal by U.S. District Court Judge Christina Snyder in a U.S. District Court of California in March 2020, and the plaintiffs are currently looking to restore their verdict on appeal. We shall wait and see what happens. Many other famous artists have been in the spotlight for unauthorized sampling. To name a few, Robin Thicke, Michael Bolton, Ed Sheeran, Bruno Mars (one of my favorites), and Beyonce (yes her too!) have sampled other artists' work and paid the price for doing so. Nonetheless, the Street Code practices, despite the Legal Code policy, continue to influence how artists create their work.

Photography – Infringement on Rights to Images
The use of images without permission is another prevalent copyright infringement issue that often happens in sports, entertainment, and business. The Legal Code for the unauthorized use of photographs made its introduction a long time ago. You need to not only understand

what the court says about specific acts being a violation but also how long it has held such an action to be illegal. Otherwise, you may be apt to believe that you are innocently doing something because so many others do it.

In 1914, the United States Court of Appeals for the Second Circuit established new common law in the case *Gross et al. v. Seligman et al.* This landmark case addressed copyright infringement based on an artist's creation of a photograph which he sold the rights to and years later created similar work that was published. In this situation, Rochiltz, the artist, created a photograph of a nude model and named the work "Grace of Youth." He sold the photograph to Gross along with the related copyrights. Two years later, the artist created another photograph using the same model positioned in an identical pose and lighting. There was a slight difference in this photograph; in that, he had the model smile with a cherry stem held between her teeth. He called this photograph, "Cherry Ripe." He sold "Cherry Ripe" to Seligman, who published it. Gross argued that the new photo infringed his copyright of the first photo. The court ruled in his favor by finding that the second photograph was an infringement upon the earlier work. The court looked at "Cherry Ripe" as a reproduction of the original work with only minor differences.

This case dates back to 1914, but the Legal Code is just as strong today as it was then. Yet, according to the Street Code, you may believe it is ok to use and reproduce photographs and digital images at any time and in any way you want. This belief is especially prevalent now because social media encourages and reinforces this behavior. Celebrities and non-celebrities alike share this belief.

You have to be mindful of blindly following the Street Code and taking images from internet sites to use for your websites or other personal objectives. We create memes with images we find online. Business owners use digital images that are not their original creation to sell products or services. Entertainers use photographs and digital images to promote parties, album singles, video content, etc. Athletes use photographs and digital images of themselves to promote their brand. Blindly following the Street Code and using photographs and digital images that are not your original creation can create big issues that can impact you legally and economically, whether you are a business owner, entertainer, or athlete.

One of the biggest issues occurs when athletes and entertainers use images of themselves taken by others even when they are not authorized to do so. Even if the picture is of you, that doesn't mean you own the right to use the image. Not understanding this critical piece of the Legal Code will put you at risk for a lawsuit—again, even if the image is of you!

ISSUE

"I cannot teach anybody anything.
I can only make them think."
- Socrates

Asked and Answered

Regardless of the piece of work that you would like to use is accessible, popular, used by others, or perfect for what is needed, there is one question that should always be asked and answered if you are not the rightful owner. Is it permissible to use another artist's work in your project?

When inquiring about using a song for sampling purposes, you may have to seek permission for two works. Depending on your project, there may be a need to request permission to use the composition (lyrics) and masters (sound recording). Knowing who to ask is essential as well. Different people or companies may have an ownership interest in one song. The problem is that the questions are never asked or asked too late. I've seen so many projects get shut down for failure to get permission. After all the blood, sweat, and tears, the project owner couldn't fulfill the regulations for approval. Other obstacles may arise, such as not being able to pay the required licensing fee or not fulfilling required obligations from multiple co-owners of a song. Worse yet, the use of the outside work may not be permitted because the copyright owner(s) did not want any affiliation with the project or project owner after review.

When inquiring about using photographs and digital images for your personal or business use, several questions should come to mind. A question you may need to ask is, "I found this picture online, can I download it and use it?" Another question you may consider is, "I paid a photographer for a photoshoot, can I use the photographs of myself as I want?" Yet another could be, "Someone took a picture of me without my consent, can they or I use the photo?" You may be saying, of course, the answer is yes; it's a photo of me. Hold that thought. These are very important answers to seek because, again, the unauthorized use of photos and digital images that someone else owns is a sure way to find yourself involved in a copyright violation claim.

The cases addressed later in this section will expose you to what happened to individuals who did not seek answers to these questions before their unauthorized use. You may be thinking, people use pictures all the time, and no one goes after them. Please know that just because a rightful owner does not exercise their rights on every use, does not mean when they decide to go after someone they can't. You don't want to end up being that someone, so don't fall for the Street Code. As you will learn in the

Right to Privacy and Trademark sections, using an image without permission can create more than one infringement violation. Not only could you be sued for copyright infringement but also for failure to obtain publicity rights and/or a trademark violation.

Industry Practice

As an attorney, I hear the same push back over and over on why there shouldn't be such great concern about intellectual property violations. Some of those remarks include, "other people do it all the time." "I've done it before, and nothing has happened to me." "It's fair use, so I have a right to do it."

Understandably, it may be hard to believe that the use of other people's work is not a big deal when we see it done all the time online. We see it on YouTube, Facebook, Instagram, Twitter, in underground music, on ads, t-shirts, and the list goes on. In other words, when the Street Code says it is alright, it must be. But that is not the case. Impermissible use of another's work is a big deal. Understanding boundaries can not only help prevent you from offending the Legal Code, but it can also empower you to fully protect your rights as an athlete, entertainer, or business owner.

RULES

"Knowledge, like air, is vital to life.
Like air, no one should be denied it."
- ***Alan Moore***

Copyright Protections

Copyright covers both published and unpublished works. What is published work? According to copyright law, establishing publication happens in several ways – distributing copies of a written work or sound recordings (phonorecords) of the work to the public, or by offering to distribute to a group of people for further distribution, use in public performance, or public display. Establishing publication can also happen through a sale or other transfer of ownership, by rental, lease, or lending.

Copyright protects original works of authorship including literary, dramatic, musical, and artistic works, such as poetry, novels, movies, songs, computer software, and architecture. Creating protection under copyright happens once the work is created and fixed in a tangible form. Copyright law clarifies "fixed" to mean work captured in a permanent form where it can be perceived or communicated for more than a short time. Writing, painting, drawing, or a recording (video, tape, or audio) are examples of works "fixed" in tangible forms.

An owner of copyrighted work possesses exclusive rights to the work, including the ability to:

1. reproduce the work (make copies);
2. create a derivative (an extension of it);
3. distribute (sell, rent, or lease);
4. perform live;
5. perform digitally; or
6. to display the copyrighted work.

An owner of copyright also has the right to prohibit others from doing any or all of the above with their work.

Because copyright protection is available once a work of authorship is created and fixed in a tangible form, you don't have to register your work to receive some protection. So yes, federal registration is optional, but having unregistered work has its limitations (discussed below). While registration may be voluntary, you will need to prove ownership if you don't register your work. In contrast, under federal registration, you may have the presumption of validity as the rightful owner if registered within a specified time.

If you register your work with the federal government through the United States Copyright Office (www.copyright.gov), you will enhance your protection. To begin with, you will have the ability to enforce your exclusive rights in federal court. You can't file an infringement claim in federal court unless you register your work. Your registration can serve as prima facie evidence (truth unless proven otherwise) that the copyright is valid, and that you are the owner as long as you complete registration before publication, or within five years from publication. Furthermore, if you register your work before someone infringes on it, or within three months after publication, you may be able to choose statutory damages (instead of proving actual damages and infringer profits), attorney fees, and costs if you win your case. Statutory damages are generally $750-$30,000 for an infringement on each work. If the court finds that your actions are intentional, you can be fined up to $150,000. If done innocently, the court can lower the damages to $200 per infringement. Lastly, federal registration can protect your work from the importation of infringing copies with the U.S. Customs and Border Protection.

Life Span
The lifespan of copyright is not indefinite. Copyright's lifespan is determined by looking at the time of its creation, or, from the registration of published or unpublished work.

The lifespan of copyright would be the life of the creator plus seventy years after the creator's death if the work was created **on or after** January 1, 1978. Any work created and <u>published or registered</u> **before** January 1, 1978, had the initial term of twenty-eight years from the date of publication with notice or from the time of registration. The registration could be renewed for another sixty-seven years after the initial term. Works created **before** January 1, 1978, that were not published or registered at the time have the same life span as works created on or after January 1, 1978.

It's important to note that a work made for hire has a separate life span. "Work for hire" means the service is being specially ordered or commissioned for the type of work permitted under copyright law for such a claim. For works made for hire, the duration of copyright is 95 years from publication or 120 years from creation, whichever is shorter (the copyright lifespan is the same for anonymous or pseudonymous works).

Losing it All

Copyright law is not something to ignore or to not take seriously. The reason legislators went through great pains to cover the ins and outs of copyright law was to protect freedom of expression and creative participation. As discussed, the law has determined what exclusive rights exist and limitations to those rights. When the Street Code practice governs over the Legal Code policy, there is a risk of losing all that you work so hard for.

Exceptions to the Rule

The general rule is to seek permission from the copyright owner directly before using their work or through the agent or company that is delegated this duty on behalf of the owner. There are exceptions and limitations to this general rule that permit use without requesting permission. However, these exemptions apply to specific circumstances. The statutory license exceptions are written in section 112-122 of the Copyright Act of 1976. The full list of limitations is available in section 107-122 of the Copyright Act of 1976 and subsequent amendments. To give a shortlist example, reproductions by libraries and archives are limitations on exclusive rights. Instructional or educational purposes under specific guidelines are limitations on exclusive rights. The most recited exception by the general public is the "fair use" doctrine.

The U.S. Copyright Office describes fair use as "a legal doctrine that promotes freedom of expression and permits the unlicensed use of copyrighted work." Consideration of the fair use defense can apply to unpublished and published work. Please note, the court determines fair use on a case by case basis. The fair use doctrine needs to be better understood by the general public before it is raised as a shield against a lawsuit.

There are factors that courts analyze when determining if the use of copyrighted work is fair use or not. Each court weighs the factors in their own way. Thus, this rule is not as black and white as it appears on paper. The general elements a court will look at are:

1. purpose and character of the use (was the work used for commercial or for nonprofit educational purposes);
2. the nature of the copyrighted work;
3. the amount and substantiality used; and
4. the effect of the use upon the potential market for or value of the copyrighted work.

Historically, in the legal community, the belief was that raising fair use was proof that an infringement had taken place. So, arguing fair use as a defense was stating that there was an admission that the infringer believed warranted forgiveness. This theory is no longer correct from a legal perspective. As the court explained in *Stephanie Lenz v. Universal Music Corp.* "... as a judicial doctrine without any statutory basis, fair use was an infringement that was excused. This is presumably why it was treated as a defense. As a statutory doctrine, however, fair use is not an infringement." In other words, after the passage of the 1976 Act, the fair use defense is not considered an admittance to an infringement. The law views fair use as a right to use. Although fair use is a right under the Legal Code, the Street Code utilizes this protection with a broad stroke. Fair use is a right that is easy to raise, but a court's outcome is more challenging to predict.

There will be more discussion about this case, the factors used to determine fair use, and the breakdown of fair use argued in court, in the following section of this guide.

APPLICATION

"Beware of the man who works hard to learn something,
learns it, and finds himself no wiser than before."
- Kurt Vonnegut

Street Code Sampling

As discussed previously, when it comes to sampling music, the Street Code warrants if you like it use it. We touched on the bad idea of getting permission after completing a project. But still, some use other artist's work without permission and wait to see if they get caught. Hopefully, that is not you! The court had something to say about this mentality in *Grand Upright Music Limited (Plaintiff) v. Warner Bros. Records (Defendant)*. The court made a strong statement about this Street Code mentality in the music industry by issuing the holding in this case that was premised on the saying, "Thou shalt not steal" and proceeded with shutting the Street Code philosophy down.

Grand Upright Music Limited filed a copyright claim to get an injunction against the defendants Marcel Hall p.k.a Biz Markie (a celebrity rap artist), his team, and Warner Bros to stop the improper and unlicensed use of the composition, "Alone Again (Naturally)." "Alone Again (Naturally)" is a composition that was written and performed on records by Raymond "Gilbert" O'Sullivan.

The defendants admitted that "the Biz Markie album 'I Need A Haircut' embodies the rap recording 'Alone Again' by using three words from Alone Again (Naturally)" composed by Gilbert.

The defendants argued they didn't know they did anything wrong and that they were not guilty of infringement. There were three things the court looked at to decide on each of the defendants' guilt or innocence. The first thing the court looked at was copies of the original copyright. The rightful owner at that time was a music company that had since dissolved. Although the company had dissolved, it vested a deed of title in the copyrights to Gilbert and the plaintiff's corporation. The second thing was the testimony of Gilbert identifying the Grand Upright Music Limited as the rightful owner. The third, and most compelling thing the court looked at were the actions of the defendants, which proved they knew what they were doing was not legitimate.

The court felt the most persuasive evidence of the defendants being aware of their wrongdoing was that, at some point, various defendants discussed getting a license. When they could not get the license, they opted to take a chance. In court, they argued their position by using the rationale of the Street Code that sampling is an act committed all the time in the music industry. The court shot back with the Legal Code by stating the following. "You would have this court believe that stealing is rampant in the music business, and for that reason, the conduct here should be excused." The court was going to make it very clear that this was an unacceptable argument. The court continued, "[t]his callous disregard for the law and for the rights of others requires not only the preliminary injunction sought by the plaintiff but also sterner measures."

When the court said the defendants should get sterner measures, they meant serious business. The court found the defendants guilty and granted the preliminary injunction sought by the plaintiffs. As a sterner measure, the court took it upon itself to refer the matter to the United States Attorney for the Southern District of New York for consideration of prosecution under criminal charges.

It's My Photograph

As discussed in the previous section, using photographs without authorization is also a widespread issue in all industries. The Street Code is if you can "Google" it, download it, save it to your device, or reshare it...then use it. If it's a picture of you, then no question, use it. Now let's look at some cases surrounding this mindset.

A copyright claim involving an athlete or entertainer usually consists of the use of an image of themselves, or, an image affiliated with their persona. However, as discussed previously in the Rules section of this guide, the owner of a copyright has certain exclusive rights. A person cannot use a work of authorship that they don't own the rights to even if the work includes their image. By now, you should know the answer to the questions presented in the Facts section previously. But, let's look at some court cases.

A recent claim was filed in court addressing the issue of an athlete using a photograph with his image. *Steven Mitchell (Plaintiff) v. Lebron James, Uninterrupted Digital Ventures, LLC, and LRMR Ventures, LLC. (Defendant)* was filed in The United States District Court in the Southern District of New York. This claim (still in its filing stage as of this writing) involves an athlete, Lebron James, using a copyrighted image where he is the subject of the photograph.

Lebron allegedly infringed on Steven's copyright ownership in a photograph he took of Lebron during in-game action. The picture captured Lebron dunking on Meyers Leonard in a Lakers vs. Heat game in Miami. Lebron re-posted this photo to his social media page without a license or consent. Steven alleges that this violated copyrights he has on the image. There was no contractual agreement between himself, LeBron, the Lakers, or the other defendants. As the photographer who took the shot, Steven owns the right to reproduce the photograph and prohibit others from doing so.

Steven filed his complaint under Section 501 of the Copyright Act because he not only had copyright generated at the creation of the work, but he also registered it with the U.S. Copyright Office and was assigned copyright number VA 2-190-180. Because Steven registered the copyright, he could file suit to enforce his exclusive rights to the photograph. According to the claim, Steven is asking the court for $150,000 for each violation raised (review the complaint about details), a statutory benefit available as a result of registering the copyright. He also believes he should receive all the profits made from the Facebook posts if any.

The court will look at two factors to determine if there was an infringement. Steven must establish 1) ownership of a valid copyright work, and 2) that the defendant violated the copyrighted work. The same factors that this court set as precedent (previous law) in *Lebbeus Woods v. Universal City Studios, Inc.,* where they held in favor of Lebbeus over Universal City Studios, Inc. for infringement of his copyright in a drawing titled "Upper Chamber."

Lebron and the defendants may argue fair use, or, they may settle out of court. We'll have to wait and see how this plays out and if the defendants can win with a fair use argument. However, remember the four elements of fair use that I laid out in the Rules section? The court will look hard at those elements, so the court's decision may or may not go in Lebron's favor. The only thing that is for sure; asking permission instead of forgiveness would have prevented a court action.

It's My Logo

In another case involving a celebrity basketball player, Kawhi Leonard filed a copyright infringement complaint against Nike, Inc. in the U.S. District Court for the Southern District of California. This time the copyrighted image is not a personal photo of him as an athlete. Instead, the image is a portrayal of a physical attribute of his. Kawhi uses a well-known logo known as the "KL2" on goods and services that are sold under his likeness. The logo is known to be significant to a personal attribute of his – his overly large hands "The Klaw.". He filed a lawsuit against Nike, alleging that Nike copyrighted his logo without his consent, and he wants to claim ownership in the "KL2" logo.

In *Kawhi Leonard (Plaintiff) v. Nike Inc. (Defendant)*, the complaint asked the court for relief on three issues:

1. a declaration that he is the sole author of the "KL2" logo,
2. his use of that logo does not infringe the rights of Nike, and
3. Nike committed fraud in its copyright application.

Kawhi argued he is the rightful and original owner of the logo. In the complaint, he traced the logo creation back to his college days during the time he played for San Diego State from 2009 to 2011. According to him, five months into his rookie season with the San Antonio Spurs, he had "refined" the logo to encompass his large hands, his initials, and his jersey number. The logo was intended to reflect Kawhi's image and likeness.

Kawhi argued that he authorized Nike to propose variations of the logo, as long as they understood that he retained ultimate control. According to the complaint, Nike made several proposals for modifications to the logo, and Kawhi finally accepted the design proposed in June 2014. He granted Nike permission to affix the modified "KL2" logo on their merchandise during the term of his endorsement agreement, which was initially signed in 2011 for three years, with a subsequent extension that would last to 2018. Kawhi said that, for the most part, he rejected Nike's suggested variations of the logo, except for the modification proposed and accepted in June 2014.

The issue here is that between 2014 and May of 2017, no one claimed federal copyright in the logo. In May 2017, the U.S. Copyright Office granted Nike's application to register the logo. On the application, Nike claimed to have owned and created the logo in 2014. This is an example of how waiting to register your copyright can become an issue! Kawhi got beaten to the punch when Nike fought back using the Legal Code. Nike covered themselves by breaking the Street Code and being the first to register the copyright in 2017.

Kawhi's failure to register a piece of work he intended to own and maintain rights before engaging in business dealings related to that work is an example of Kawhi operating under the Street Code. The Street Code has set a standard that downplays protecting personal property. Informal conversations take place during business deals when formal written agreements should be a priority. A friendly discussion is fine, but the person who stands to lose it all should not move on that discussion until his or her expectations are agreed upon and enforceable. When a business relationship is going well, and everyone is happy to work together, details surrounding an agreement get overlooked, or worse, they are not taken into consideration at all. Written agreements are not put into place when they should be, or people rely on friendly texts or emails, which can be helpful, but should not be relied on. These informal communications are not useful if there is a contract in place that overrides those previous informal verbal and written communications.

Nike argued Kawhi had a contractual obligation to create or assist in creating for their brand, and the "KL2" logo was a work made for hire. What was the result of having this "work for hire" terminology in Kawhi's contract?

In addition to Nike's 2017 copyright registration, Nike was able to assert ownership in the logo under the 2011 endorsement deal with Kawhi and its subsequent extension – that's what!

After the court reviewed the facts and evidence against the law, it ruled Nike is the rightful owner of the "KL2" logo, and any unauthorized use by Kawhi or anyone else would be an infringement. The U.S. District Judge Michael W. Mosman expressed, "It's not merely a derivative work of the sketch itself. I do find it to be new and significantly different from the design."

I come across these "work for hire" catch-all terms in athlete endorsement deals all the time. Work for hire language is a standard provision in these types of contracts and not one to be taken so lightly. Kawhi's best protection could have been to amend the terms in his endorsement contract with Nike. To be specific, he could have addressed that any collaboration on his logo, or anything else he owned before working with Nike, was not to be included in the work for hire clause. He could have added terms to his contract, explicitly addressing collaboration toward the final logo, including original work and any subsequent new work. Not to mention, he could have registered copyright in the "KL2" logo once it was complete to enhance his protection and benefits that come with it. He had at least three years to file for a federal copyright registration to protect his interest in the logo as Nike didn't attempt to register the copyright itself until 2017.

Story Theft

The film industry is another industry subject to frequent copyright infringement. A lot of inspiration comes from film, and sometimes that inspiration can walk a fine line between original creativity and copyright infringement. Too often, creatives submit unprotected scripts for review or as solicitations to individuals they want to work with. Operating by the Street Code of sharing without caring will make life very hard for a creative in the long run.

Fighting a story theft case in court is already problematic. Therefore, it is best to create a scenario that gives you a fighting chance. By registering federal copyright in your work, you will gain the expanded benefits provided under the law. Creating and disseminating a written agreement stating what the intentions for sharing are, and what the expectations are if the story is used, increases your protection even more (more on this in the Contracts section). It may also help to have an attorney or agent send such an agreement on your behalf. Most production companies require an agent or attorney must do just that.

The case, *Jerome C. Metcalf and Laurie Metcalf (Plaintiffs) v. Bochco Steven Productions, a corporation; CBS Entertainment, Inc., a corporation*; and *Michael Warren (Defendants),* shows just how tough the fight can be. In this lawsuit, Jerome and Laurie (the 'Metcalfs') fought to overturn a previous ruling that Bochco Steven Productions ('Bochco') and CBS were not liable for copyright infringement of their script.

In 1989, the Metcalfs conceived a story about a county hospital in inner-city Los Angeles and the struggles of its predominantly black staff. They formed a corporation, CCA, to develop the idea into a full-length motion picture. Jerome discussed the idea with Michael, a friend who is an actor that starred in television shows produced by Bochco.

The Metcalfs wrote their treatment and titled it 'Give Something Back' and gave it to Michael. Michael told the Metcalfs he would share the script with Bochco. Michael later followed up and told Jerome that Bochco liked the treatment but had declined to use it because he was busy with other projects. The Metcalfs' company CCA then hired another author to write a screenplay based on the treatment. Michael reviewed this work, now titled 'As Long As They Kill Themselves,' and submitted it to Bochco. Michael reported back near the end of 1991 that Bochco still lacked time to develop the content. The Metcalfs revised the screenplay and retitled it one more time to 'About Face.'

In 1992, they pitched the work to Bochco (again via Michael) and CBS. CBS explained that it had another hospital series in development at the time. On January

16, 2000, the television series 'City of Angels' premiered on CBS. The pilot and first episode were produced and written by Bochco, starred Michael, and appeared to be similar to the idea and the screenplay the Metcalf's shared with Michael.

The court applied an objective test to determine if there were substantial similarities between the two works. The scripts had to meet the substantial similarities test and could not be merely similar. The court examined the plot, themes, dialogue, mood, setting, pace, characters, and sequence of events of the two scripts.

To consider the sequence and similarity, the courts compared both scripts, the Metcalfs' script, and the script for the 'City of Angels' pilot and first episode. Both settings were inner-city Los Angeles with mostly black staff. Both scripts dealt with issues of poverty, race relations, and urban blight. The main characters in both scripts were young, good-looking, muscular black surgeons who grew up in the neighborhood where the hospital was located. Both scripts described the surgeon's struggle to choose between the financial benefits of private practice and the emotional rewards of working in the inner-city. Both scripts had the main character, romantically involved with young professional women. In both scripts, the main character arrived at the hospital and developed a strong attraction to the hospital administrator, the new relationship flourished and culminated in a kiss. Both scripts also describe the strain in the new relationship when the administrator observes a display of physical intimacy between the main character and his primary love interest. The administrators in both scripts are in their thirties, once married but are now single, without children, and devoted to their career and the hospital. In both works, a Hispanic politician opposed the hospital's bid for reaccreditation.

In response to the infringement claim, the defendants, Bochco, CBS, and Michael, argued copyright protects the expression of ideas and not the ideas themselves. The court responded that the particular sequence in which an author strings a significant number of unprotectable elements together, can itself become a protectable element.

Under these circumstances, finding favor for the Metcalfs was a slam dunk because so many elements were the same. The court expressed the "totality of the similarities ... goes beyond the necessities of the ... theme and belies any claim of literary accident." Elements that could have stood weak alone, as a whole, stood strong, and the Metcalfs were able to satisfy the court's test undeniably.

Aside from the main reason for pointing out this case, which is how tough a legal battle can be for story theft on a copyright claim alone, I want to note that the Metcalfs initially filed a complaint in state court. The defendants had it removed to federal court. The Metcalfs would not have been able to fight this in federal court if they hadn't registered the work. Had they not filed the copyright, the removal to federal court could have been a strategy used by the Defendants to dismiss their copyright claim. In this case, the Metcalfs followed the Legal Code and were able to litigate their issue. To reiterate the discussion made earlier about the benefits of registering federal copyright, although registration may not be mandatory, it is highly suggested.

Each court may apply the "substantial similarity test" differently. Some may do so in a less strict manner than others. Therefore, you need to be prepared for the highest standard if you ever find yourself in this situation. Story thieves can make enough changes to the content to prevail on this test. Creating a contract prior to sharing your work with anyone could go a long way to protect your interests in court.

The Application of Fair Use as a Defense

Earlier, I touched on fair use as a right afforded by law. However, I also mentioned there is no clear rule on the weighing of the four elements determining fair use. As a reminder, the four elements used to determine fair use are:

1. purpose and character of the use (was the work used for commercial or for nonprofit educational purposes);
2. the nature of the copyrighted work;
3. the amount and substantiality used; and
4. the effect of the use upon the potential market for or value of the copyrighted work.

Prevailing on the fair use defense could depend on the judge, the state the complaint was filed in, and a variety of other factors. Here are a few cases with different outcomes based on the court's weighing of the fair use factors.

Innocent Act

In, *Austris A. Wihtol (Plaintiff and Appellant) v. Nelson Crow (Defendant and Appellee)*, the court made it clear on how it felt about including innocent intent in the fair use argument. Austris is the copyright owner of the musical composition, 'My God and I.' He alleged that Nelson infringed on his work because he made and distributed an unauthorized arrangement of the work. The lower court ruled that defendant's reproduction of the work was "fair use" because he did not intend to commit copyright infringement. Austris appealed to the district court's ruling.

In reversing the district court, the appellate court held that "innocent intent" has no bearing on a fair use analysis. The court stated: "[w]hatever may be the breadth of the doctrine of 'fair use,' it is not conceivable to us that the copying of all, or substantially all, of a copyrighted song can be held to be a 'fair use' merely because the infringer had no intent to infringe." The takeaway, the case was argued in two courts where the lower court took into consideration the innocence argument, and the higher court said innocence had absolutely no bearing on the analysis. As you see, the outcome can depend on many factors, including the four elements of the rule. But I must say, the second court got it right. Innocence is not one of the four elements. Innocent intent may be considered in determining the damages owed, but it does not excuse the infringement.

Takedown Notice

The Street Code mentality not only applies to individual creatives, but it also applies to corporations that handle business in a manner that ignores the Legal Code. In *Stephanie Lenz (Appellants) v. Universal Music Corp. (Appellees)*, the court addressed what the copyright owner's legal duty is concerning fair use.

Stephanie posted a video on YouTube with her family that had Prince song playing in the background for 20 seconds. YouTube removed her video after receiving a takedown notice from Universal. Stephanie sued

Universal for falsely representing that the video infringed copyright held by Prince.

For an owner of the copyright to issue a takedown notice on a user-generated site, such as YouTube, the owner must determine that the use of the work does not qualify as fair use. If the owner determines in good faith that the use is an infringement, they may proceed with the takedown notice under the Digital Millennium Copyright Act (DMCA). The court stated, "[t]o be clear. If a copyright holder ignores or neglects our unequivocal holding that it must consider fair use before sending a takedown notification, it is liable for damages under § 512(f)."

Section 512(f) provides for the recovery of "any damages, including costs and attorney's fees, incurred by the alleged infringer ... who is injured by such misrepresentation, as the result of the service provider relying upon such misrepresentation in removing or disabling access to the material or activity claimed to be infringing....17 U.S.C. § 512(f)." The court went on to explain "if, however, a copyright holder forms a subjective good faith belief the allegedly infringing material does not constitute fair use, we are in no position to dispute the copyright holder's belief even if we would have reached the opposite conclusion. A copyright holder who pays lip service to the consideration of fair use by claiming it formed a good faith belief when there is evidence to the contrary is still subject to § 512."

To translate this explanation. The court is saying copyright owners have to look into the specific use with an honest intention to consider whether it falls under fair use. It is the copyright holder's discretion to take action as they choose from there. If they feel it is infringing, the court will not go against their good faith belief (right or wrong). They will not be liable for a claim for misrepresentation under 17 U.S.C §512(f).

Universal lost this case because its argument suggested that it was too risky to take time to consider if Stephanie's video fell under fair use. They argued that copyright owners might lose the ability to respond rapidly if they took the time to look at whether fair use was in play. Universal believed that if copyright owners must review potential infringements to check fair use before issuing takedown notices, it could hurt them. This blatant admittance was evidence they didn't give a good faith effort in considering fair use. Consequently, the court ruled in favor of Stephanie.

This information could be helpful for those who argue fair use for internet activity, but it also illustrates how fair use is still not as cut and dry as other areas of copyright law. What if Universal did take the time to review if Stephanie's video fell under fair use? Universal could have said they did and found that it didn't fall under fair use. According to 17 U.S.C §512(f) cited by the court, the court would not have pushed back. It was Universal's blatant admission that moved in Stephanie's favor.

Online Photograph

An analysis of fair use in a copyright claim arising out of unauthorized use of a photograph is quite different. The four factors of the fair use analysis were applied in this context in *Russell Brammer (Plaintiff) v. Violent Hues Productions, LLC (Defendant)*. Russell is a photographer who shot a time-lapse photograph of the Adams Morgan neighborhood in Washington, D.C., and posted the image on several image-sharing websites and his website. He added the phrase "© All rights reserved" beneath the photograph.

Violent Hues Productions, a film festival organizer, used a cropped version of Russell's photograph on its website alongside information about things to do in the D.C. area. That website promoted the Northern Virginia International Film and Music Festival, a revenue-generating event. Russell contacted Violent Hues to request compensation for the unauthorized use. Violent Hues removed the photograph from its website but refused to compensate Russell. Russell initiated a copyright infringement action. Violent Hues raised the fair use

In reviewing the elements of the defense, the court noted the following:

The first factor, <u>purpose and character of the use</u>, weighed against fair use because the use was not transformative. Meaning the use did not transform the old work into something new that gave it a different meaning or purpose. Violent Hues used the photograph for its content, that is, to depict the Adams Morgan neighborhood. Violent Hues said its use provided film festival attendees with "information" about the Adams Morgan neighborhood. Therefore, it was for educational purposes. In response, the court said this use would not be hindered if Violent Hues had complied with Russell's copyright and paid to license the image. The use of the photograph to illustrate a website promoting a for-profit festival is considered a commercial use.

The second factor, <u>the nature of the copyrighted work</u>, also weighed against fair use. The court concluded that Russell's photograph was a "stylized image, with vivid colors and a bird's-eye view" infused with "creative choices" that entitled it to "thick" copyright protection.

The third factor, <u>the amount and substantiality of the work used</u>, weighed against fair use. Violent Hues used roughly half the photograph, removing only the negative space and keeping the most expressive features.

The fourth factor, <u>the effect of the use on the potential market for or value of the work</u>, also weighed against fair use. The court applied a presumption of market harm because Violent Hues use was commercial and not transformative. Violent Hues' website did not generate direct revenue or run advertising. But Violent Hues is a limited liability company, and it used the photo on its website to promote a for-profit film festival. Russell introduced evidence showing that he twice licensed the photograph – a licensing market that would be dampened if Violent Hues conduct were widespread.

Considering the four factors together, the court concluded that "the copying here fails the 'ultimate test' of fair use." Anytime you decide to use a picture, or if someone uses a photo of yours under the guise of fair use, keep this case in mind.

Film Parody

Contrasting the previous case, let's look at how a court analyzed the four factors of fair use in a copyright claim for a video and came to the opposite conclusion. In *Brownmark Films, LLC (Plaintiff) v. Comedy Partners and MTV Networks (Defendants),* Brownmark filed a lawsuit alleging copyright infringement. The basis of the claim was related to a music video they owned that went viral. The defendants replicated the video on an episode of their animated sitcom "South Park." The South Park episode was titled "Canada on Strike." It had one of the characters, the naive "Butters Stotch," record an internet video in hopes of making money on the internet. The video of Butters singing the central lines of the original video lasted for fifty-eight seconds of the approximately twenty-five-minute episode, and it also copied parts of the Brownmark video.

The court analyzed the four-factors in the following manner:

It was easy for the court to see that the South Park episode's purpose and character of use were for the defendants to use parts of the Brownmark's video to lampoon the recent craze in our society of watching video clips on the internet. The South Park episode takes the original work. It uses elements of the video to make fun of the original video and to comment on a bizarre social trend solidifying the South Park episode as a classic parody. The purpose weighed in favor of fair use.

The court held that the nature of the copyrighted work was not particularly helpful to the court because the South Park episode included an imitation of, and not use of, the real video. Therefore, this factor was not relevant to the weighting.

The court held the substantiality of the copyrighted work used in the South Park episode was relatively insubstantial. Just enough words were used to conjure up the original video, but it did not mirror the original video. This weighed in favor of fair use.

Lastly, the court determined there was little risk that the derivative work in question would somehow <u>usurp the market demand</u> for the original work. Therefore, this element weighed in favor of fair use.

Based on the weighing of the four factors, the court concluded that the defendants' use of the music video in the South Park episode "Canada on Strike" was "fair."

CONCLUSION

"Knowledge comes, but wisdom lingers."
- **Alfred Lord Tennyson**

In conclusion, copyright is an important concept to understand and respect. While copyright protection in the United States exists from the moment the original work of authorship is tangible, that protection is limited. Enhanced legal protection only comes from federal registration. Remember what copyright protects and what it doesn't. Copyright protects an original work of authorship fixed in a tangible form. However, it doesn't protect ideas (unless a string of ideas create unique work), methods, titles, names, slogans, and so forth. You can view the Copyright Act, codified in Title 17, for the full list.

Under certain circumstances, the Legal Code does protect the right to use copyrighted work to share newsworthy information, in teaching, research, or for other reasons listed in the code which are not considered infringing acts. Be aware that what would generally fall under protection for limited purposes can get entangled in uses that are not protected, and there could be severe consequences if you violate someone else's rights.

Remember the Violent Hues case? Although the production company used the photograph for educational purposes, the court weighed the fair use elements to come to their conclusion considering Violent Hues' use of the photograph as commercial use and the owner's history of licensing the photograph. As a result, the court found for the plaintiff, the owner of the copyright.

It's Not Black or White

One of the most discussed and acclaimed protections under the statutory provisions of the Legal Code is fair use. As we discussed, fair use is a legal doctrine that promotes freedom of expression by permitting the unlicensed use of copyright-protected works in certain circumstances. Overcoming the four-prong analysis in court is not as black and white as it would appear to be written in the copyright exception provision.

Furthermore, as pointed out in the cases in the Application section of this guide, the fair use analysis will be applied differently based on the type of violation. Is the subject matter a photo, video, or takedown notice? Additionally, the outcome of the fair use analysis may be impacted by the state the case is filed in, the court the issue is tried in, the attorney(s) litigating, or the judge or jury deciding the case. How fair use is measured depends on what it is being measured against. Unless you sought legal advice, or for some reason you know that it is absolutely permissible to use another's work, it may be best to ask permission first.

Levels of Protection

Within one piece of work, there can be many levels of protection a person can seek under the Legal Code. For example, an image may contain content with different levels of protectable interest. The image could be protected under copyright, trademark, or right to privacy law. We have not discussed trademark or right to privacy protections yet, so I won't say too much here and will leave you to explore those sections of this guide. I will say, leaving your work unprotected or neglecting to protect your work to the fullest extent could forfeit your ownership. The Kawhi copyright case is an excellent example of what can happen if you don't cover all of your bases.

We will discuss trademarks next, but I want to mention that Kawhi did register a federal trademark for the "KL2" logo (serial numbers 87678944, 87678949, and 87678958). Unfortunately, Nike's copyright in the logo trumped Kawhi's trademark rights. Although Kawhi's trademark sought to prevent public confusion regarding the source of the good or service bearing the mark, Nike's copyright, on the other hand, protected the image of the logo itself. Consequently, Kawhi's continued use of the logo as a trademark would still constitute copyright infringement. The judgment against Kawhi allowed Nike to prevent him from using the copyrighted logo, effectively preventing Kawhi's use of the logo as a trademark for his products. You can see how seeking both legal protections for the "KL2" logo trademark, and copyright could have made things turn out differently – that is, if he covered his basis contractually as well.

Other People Do It

The Street Code encourages the far-reaching argument echoed among potential violators, "Everyone does it." How many times have you seen the disclaimer "I do not own the rights to this music" for videos posted online by individuals who were not authorized to use the music playing? Posting this disclaimer does not negate the fact that it is an infringement. To the contrary, it is an admittance of violating someone's right. Just because others may not get caught, or a copyright owner does not enforce their rights against some individuals in every instance, does not mean you will not get caught or that a copyright owner will not enforce their rights against you.

For example, the filing of the lawsuit against Lebron shocked a lot of people. I'm willing to bet he was probably shocked too. Some may think that a photographer should be glad that a highly celebrated person reposts their picture, and a lot of photographers may be. However, in this instance, Steven decided to enforce his right to file a lawsuit to prohibit the unauthorized use of his photograph. Steven exercised his rights contrary to the "other people do it" mentality of the Street Code.

CODE V. CODE
TRADEMARK

Street Code v. Legal Code

United States (2020)

FACTS

"I'm not saying I'm gonna change the world,
but I guarantee that I will spark the brain
that will change the world."
- **Tupac Shakur**

Trademark Confusion

Trademark is an area of intellectual property that touches all three industries in the same manner. A mark identifies the source of a product (trademark) or service (service mark). Many use the term trademark when referring to both products and services, and that's ok. For simplicity,

I will use the term trademark or "mark." For clarity, a trademark identifies and distinguishes goods produced by one seller from another seller. Similar to a trademark, a service mark identifies and distinguishes services rendered by one provider from similar services provided by another provider. The purpose of distinguishing and identifying the source of the product or service is to prevent consumer confusion.

Whether the source of the product or service is an entertainer, athlete, or business owner, it is important to understand the basic knowledge of the trademark Legal Code. In my experience, most people confuse and interchange the term trademark with copyright or patent, but these terms are very different and offer different protections. As addressed earlier in this guide, copyright prohibits others from copying, using, distributing, displaying, or performing a copyrighted work. A patent, on the other hand, is a government license giving a right or title of an invention to the inventor or rights holder. A patent excludes others from making, using, or selling that invention.

It is not surprising these terms confuse most people. I've heard attorneys mix up these areas of intellectual property law. I recall a time when I was a panelist on a Women in Film and Media panel, and a gentleman in the audience asked a question about patenting his script. The attorney responded that she encouraged him to do so and that she provides this service for her clients all the time. Unless the film script is an invention, describes methods of operation or systems, a patent would be the incorrect protection. The gentleman was more than likely thinking about copyright. Moral of the story, be careful who you get advice from. Make sure they are a practicing attorney in these areas. Trademark issues typically arise from a lack of understanding of the differences between trademark and other protections.

Protection and Ownership

A trademark protects a design, word, recognizable sign, name – or even a smell or sound. As an athlete, entertainer, or entrepreneur, you should familiarize yourself with trademarking if you want to increase the value of your brand. If for nothing else, you should become familiar with trademark protections to avoid violating someone else's mark. A trademark can be a tremendous financial asset to an established brand. Recently, there has been an uptick in athletes and entertainers expressing interest in trademarking, but that has not always been the case.

HISTORY

"Not everything that is faced can be changed,
but nothing can be changed until it is faced."
- ***James Baldwin***

Limited Rights – Common Law

For hundreds of years, images, designs, sounds, names, symbols, and so forth, have been regularly used for promotional strategies in advertisements, movies, music, books, newspapers, and other commercial media. However, what is considered protectable property was not always the extensive list that we have today.

Before federal trademark protection was available, trademarks were protected under common law. Common law only gives limited rights to the owner of the trademark; for instance, under common law, protections are limited to geographic areas in which the trademark is used. Additional trademark protection is provided under a state registration. Just as common law protection is limited to geographic areas, state registration is limited to the state of registration. The main difference is that by registering a state trademark, you can put people on notice of your ownership by being listed in the state's database.

The creation of the United States Patent and Trademark Office (USPTO) allowed for the federal registration of trademarks, which offered broader protection than common law, including the expansion of protection beyond the geographical area in which a trademark was used.

Expanded Protection – Lanham Act and the USPTO

Trademark protection was not heavily considered or understood outside of the manufacturing industry. It wasn't until the 1840's that the first trademark lawsuit arose in the United States.

For decades, issues of trademark infringement were considered civil cases that took place in equity law courts and some state courts. These courts only ruled on monetary fines or injunctions (a ruling that requires a person to stop infringing). The court issued fines were calculated based on the profits generated as a result of the infringement on the trademark. The amount of profit gained could be difficult to prove and, at times, too small to be worth the cost and time needed to challenge the infringement in court.

Legal institutions and the courts continued to struggle to develop trademark laws in the 1870s. Interestingly, the most significant obstacle in the progression of trademark law ended up being the U.S. Constitution. In the late 1870s, an attempt to create federal trademark law failed to overcome constitutional challenges. In *B. Leidersdorf v. J.G. Flint* (1878), the judge ruled that "the maker of a trademark is neither an author nor an inventor and a trademark is neither writing nor a discovery within the meaning and intent of the constitutional clause in question." In translation, the court ruled that the trademark law was unconstitutional.

In 1946, after several attempts to revamp the trademark law, Congress passed the Lanham Act. The Lanham Act defines federal trademark protections, governs federal registration rules, and gives authority to the USPTO to oversee the process of obtaining a federal registration. Consequently, by the end of the century, the courts not only expanded the borders of protection from a geographic area to a national reach but also what could be protected.

Initially, trademark protection was considered a practice for the manufacturing industry. Trademark law applied to specific marks on manufactured goods to prevent other manufacturers and distributors from using the same mark to sell similar products. By the late twentieth century, trademark protection went from protecting the actual mark from being duplicated to prohibiting any close imitation of the mark. As trademark law continued to evolve, the law expanded protection against competitors and non-competitors alike. Eventually, we got to where we are today, the expansion of trademark protection to prevent confusion of marks that are identical or similar used by providers in the same industry.

Even though trademark law evolved to include trademarks other than those held by manufacturing companies, the public mindset did not. The Street Code belief that trademarks were not important to individual entertainers, athletes, or small businesses remained.

Cultural Impact

After the expansion of trademark protection, organized sports teams, entertainment conglomerates, and large businesses capitalized on these protections by including intellectual property clauses in their contracts. Despite the changes in who and what trademark law grew to protect, trademark law's early roots in big business seemed to have had a cultural impact on the athlete, entertainer, and small business owners. For a long while, there remained a lack of understanding and interest in how trademarking applied to them. The major players remained at the forefront of demanding intellectual property protection by securing ownership in the rights of others, including their name, image, and likeness, especially of athletes and entertainers. Even though these athletes, entertainers, and entrepreneurs were providers of products and services, they didn't seem to have an interest in obtaining a federal trademark. There is starting to be a shift in the interest in pursuing trademarks to maintain ownership as more small businesses are expressing interest in protecting their brands, and celebrities are eager to capitalize on their reputation. Arguably though, not as much of a shift as there should be.

Owning a registered trademark should accomplish two things. First, it should make it easy for a consumer to identify the source of the product or service. Second, it should prevent impermissible use that would somehow appear to affiliate the owner's product or service with an unauthorized user. The first objective is universally understood and respected. The second objective is not always met as entrepreneurs and individuals in the sport and entertainment industries do not always take the necessary precautions to protect their marks and brand. Similar to how the Street Code governed copyrights, the Street Code established a common practice in these industries of capitalizing off of other people's brands as one saw fit with an expectation of little or no repercussions. You will see examples of the consequences of reliance on the Street Code in my discussion of a few cases in the Application section.

ISSUE

"Change the way you look at things
and the things you look at change."
- **Wayne W. Dyer**

Coexisting Brands

Even though common law extends limited protection for a trademark, some issues can arise with unregistered marks such as coexisting brands. If you are running a business in California, and another person is running a business in New York, and you both have the same brand name who owns it? Who has the right to expand their territory if you both decide to do so? What if you have been operating your business for years and decided to register your trademark, but someone else has registered a similar one to yours, providing the same product? These are some of the issues that the trademark law encourages you to think about. If you don't think about these things, you can run into many issues before registering your trademark. You could find yourself coexisting with another brand, in a legal battle, or applying for non-registrable marks.

Although you should be able to answer many of these questions and understand the protections a registered trademark provides after reviewing the Rules section, you are probably thinking, "I should hire a lawyer. Right?" That is good thinking because a trademark application is a legal proceeding. It may be in your best interest to at least seek counsel from an attorney to advise and guide you through the filing process. The USPTO has filing requirements that you must meet to achieve a successful outcome. Each requirement will establish whether you have a legally protectable and federally registerable mark.

RULES

"Show me the asset, and I'll show you its price."
- Robert Black

Legal Proceeding

The trademark application process is a legal proceeding governed by U.S. law. Like copyright law, you do not have to register your trademark to establish you have a trademark. Also, like copyright law, your mark will only have limited protection if you do not register it for federal protection. Unlike copyright law, you can litigate an infringement on your unregistered trademark through common law statute relating to unfair competition. You can exercise these legal rights in local or state court, but your rights to your trademark will only apply to the geographic areas in which you operate. The only two ways that you could litigate in federal court is if the person who violated your rights lives in a different state and the dispute is more than $75,000, or if there is a federal question or a need for interpretation of the Lanham Act that needs to be resolved.

In applying for a registered trademark, your application must meet many legal requirements, including, and most importantly, the mark must be able to identify the goods and services produced and the source from which they come. The mark may not qualify for registration if, for example, it contains words used in common everyday language or if approving the filing of the mark would have a negative effect when stopping other people from using it.

What is a federally registrable or legally protectable mark? The USPTO weighs the strength of the mark by looking at its uniqueness. They base their decision on whether the mark is generic, descriptive, suggestive, fanciful, or arbitrary (for a full understanding on these terms visit USPTO.gov). The USPTO also reviews if the mark will cause other issues with its registration. Possible concerns could be:

1. submitting geographic terms. Geographic terms are generally descriptive of the place of origin;

2. submitting a surname. Others who have the same last name may want to use that name to refer to themselves and their products and services;

3. submitting foreign language terms. The USPTO translates any non-English words into English before comparing trademarks to look for a similar mark registered in different languages or to see if the translated word would result in a weak trademark because it is descriptive in English;

4. submitting obscene language. The USPTO can restrict marks that may be offensive to the public;

5. title of a single book or movie;
6. someone's image and likeness without proper consent;
7. a decorative or ornamental matter; and lastly
8. the likelihood of confusion with another mark that already exists. The USPTO reviews similarity to existing marks and whether the mark applied for is in the same or relatable market.

Individuals living in the U.S. can file on their behalf or on behalf of their business. Otherwise, an applicant must have an attorney complete the application for them. A non-attorney cannot prepare the application for registration, and they cannot represent you before the USPTO; neither can a foreign attorney.

To Register or Not to Register

Registering a trademark has a variety of benefits, including 1) the ability to bring a federal trademark suit, 2) notice to the public of your ownership rights in the mark, 3) the right to use the federal trademark registration symbol ®, and 4) assistance in obtaining foreign registration abroad.

As mentioned previously, trademarks not registered with the USPTO have protections through common law or state registration. You can register a trademark with your state through its state trademark registration process, which is less expensive than a federal registration. The filing process varies from state to state. State registration will put people on notice that you exist by listing your trademark in the state's searchable database. It will also establish a record for you regarding the date you began using your mark. This can be very helpful if you are unable to register with the USPTO at the time. And again, you can enforce your rights in local or state court.

Federal registration is superior to common law and state registration when considering damages for the infringement on your trademark. The court presumes the holder of a registered mark is the rightful owner. The burden is placed on the other side to prove otherwise. What does this all mean? Registering a trademark puts you in the best legal position to protect your asset.

Federal registration doesn't guarantee that you will not have to coexist with a brand that has the same trademark or that you won't find yourself in a legal battle. If someone has a mark that is the same or similar to yours and was providing a service or product in the same market before you used your mark, they may be able to stop you from using your unregistered or registered mark in their geographical area. A court could rule that you both have to exist within your territory. That is why it is important to hire a trademark attorney to do a clearance search (unless you know how) before deciding on your trademark and registering it. If you are the first to use and register your trademark, you will have national protection. As long as your registration is legitimate and you don't abandon it or allow your mark to become a generic term, your trademark will become incontestable after five years if your file the appropriate declaration. In other words, it will become immune from challenge.

APPLICATION

"You can fool some people sometimes,
but you can't fool all the people all the time."
-Bob Marley

A Business Mark

As a business owner, you need to choose a trademark that identifies who you are and what you have to offer to the world. It is of equal importance that the mark is developed as a result of a well thought out process. The Street Code may encourage you to focus on marketing strategy well before you even consider a legal strategy. Under the Street Code, the initial goal is to make something look good and sound good to attract consumers. To get up and running and sell products or services and announce to the world that you have arrived. A famous entrepreneur mantra that many of us business owners have heard is "just start." Thinking through the legal aspect of the plan is something that many, including yourself, may believe can come later, if at all. On the contrary, a legal strategy, including the evaluation of protections for your brand provided under the Legal Code, could be a great benefit if taken into consideration throughout the business development process.

If the legal implications of early decisions are not of concern in the foundational stages of the development process, legal problems can take shape from the very beginning without you even knowing it. For example, if you choose a brand name that is descriptive or generic, it can have serious implications for you down the road. A common approach many entrepreneurs take in selecting a brand name or identifier as a representation of their business is to choose something that simply describes what they are selling. For example, someone may choose "Big Mike T'shisrts" or "The bicycle shop." Brands such as these could be considered descriptive or generic. If you choose a mark for your brand that is descriptive, you may end up sharing it with a competitor because you will need five years to establish a required secondary meaning. If you choose a mark for your brand that the USPTO considers generic, you may end up sharing that mark with the world because it will never get approved for registration. If implementing a legal strategy was done early in the process, these common mistakes can be identified, and more than likely, the headache a generic or descriptive mark could bring could be prevented. A legal strategy could put you in the best position to adhere to the Legal Code and meet the requirements of the USPTO when establishing your brand.

What happens when the business owner does not think of the brand identifier of their business as their first legal dealing? The creator may end up putting blood, sweat, and tears into a building a company tethered to a mark that can't meet federal trademark protection rules. Worse yet, they may discover they are providing a service or product in the same or related field as a competitor, who uses the same or similar mark.

The case *Fleischmann Distilling Corp. (Plaintiff) v. Maier Brewing Co. (Defendant)* is a good illustration of what can happen when the Legal Code is not taken into consideration during the development of a mark.

Fleischmann Distilling imported scotch into the U.S. under the name "Black & White," which had been trademarked by them. Maier Brewing sold a product called "Black & White" beer. Fleischmann Distilling sued Maier Brewing for trademark infringement. The court based its decision on the likelihood of confusion standard to determine the outcome. Meaning they posed the question, "Would the ordinary purchaser, buying with ordinary caution, be misled?" The court remarked that the "Black & White" brand identifier, although used by two different businesses, were identical names branding different products in the same market. Though the products were not in direct competition – scotch versus beer – both products were alcoholic beverages. The court explained that consumers might think that there is a connection between the creators of the products, therefore, confusing the buyers. Thus, the court ruled that Maier Brewing was infringing.

Protecting a brand goes beyond the registration of the trademark with the USPTO. Protecting a brand on a federal level depends on how the owner of the trademark continues to use and protect it. Often entrepreneurs get comfortable running a business to create a product or provide a service and put far less energy and effort into protecting their trademark from the use by others, and even more importantly, protecting the mark from becoming generic. This behavior is described as "failing to safe harbor your billboard to the world." Your mark is your billboard. It announces to the world that you are the source of the product or service. Trademarks once regarded as strong by the USPTO can become generic and weak if not policed. What happens if your mark is considered generic? It will not be protected. The court in *Abercrombie & Fitch Co. (Plaintiff) v. Hunting World, Inc. (Defendant)* explains how a generic mark is treated.

Abercrombie owned a trademark in "Safari" for certain types of clothes. Hunting World used the mark on its products and newsletter. Abercrombie sued for trademark infringement. The court dismissed this part of the claim because it ruled "Safari" had come to be a generic word known as a class of goods relating to going on actual safaris. Consequently, Hunting World was able to use on their clothing.

Athlete Name and Likeness

Athletes should consider trademarking their name or likeness if they are in the business of providing a service or product. If you are an athlete, you are more than just your physical talent. You are a business too. What if someone else wants to trademark your name or likeness? What if you want to trademark a famous athlete name for a product you sell? This is not uncommon. There are times others try to capitalize on the likeness of a well-known person. It is important to note that applying for a mark by submitting someone else's name or likeness without consent is grounds for barring registration. The USPTO reviews translations of words in other languages to see if the word correlates to the name of a person other than the applicant.

What if you are a U.S. athlete, and someone in another country wants to register your name in their country? The USPTO is for U.S. protection only. Foreign countries may have completely different processes for trademark registration. Therefore, it may be a good idea to look into how you can protect your brand outside of the U.S. Sometimes, foreign businesses trademark conflict with trademarks registered in the U.S. There was a case that recently addressed an alleged trademark infringement based on a foreign translation of a famous athlete's name. The case is *Michael Jordan v. Qiaodan Sport* filed in the Supreme People's Court of China. It was China, not our USPTO, that was able to, and did, protect Michael's name.

In 1997, a Fujian company created a sportswear line to sell sporting goods to Chinese consumers. It registered its business name as Qiaodan Sports Company, Limited. The company continued to add to its inventory of trademarks and filed more than 100 applications. One of those filings was for a logo of a basketball player jumping. It included the number 23. Another one of the trademark applications filed by Qiaodan Sports included the Chinese characters 乔丹 or the pinyin word "Qiaodan."

The name "Qiaodan" started being used in 1986, appearing in Chinese newspapers and on television broadcasts of NBA games long before the formation of Qiaodan Sports. The Chinese used Qiaodan as a rough transliteration of Michael's surname, Jordan. Michael sued Quiodan in 2012, and in 2020, in the Supreme People's Court—the highest court in China. The court ruled in favor of Michael after an eight-year-long trademark battle with the Chinese company. As a result of the verdict, Qiaodan Sports cannot use the Chinese translation of Michael's surname, Qiao Dan.

Although Michael won his infringement claim regarding his name, Quiodan Sports was able to continue using the logo of a silhouetted basketball player that "has simi-larities with the 'Jumpman' logo used by Nike to promote the 'Air Jordan' line of sports shoes." If the "Jumpman" logo were used without permission in the U.S., the USPTO would more than likely have prevented its use. As you see, a foreign trademark can conflict with your trademark in the U.S., and you may have no recourse to bar its use in a foreign country.

Even if he wanted to, Michael wouldn't be able to bring the lawsuit for infringement on the logo. If there were an issue, it would be Nike that could file the com-plaint. Why is that? Most people refer to the Jumpman or Air Jordan as being affiliated with the Michael Jordan brand. And, technically, they are. However, Nike owns the brand and is the rightful copyright and trademark owner of the Jumpman image and logo and the Air Jordan mark. The corporation owns the "Air Jordan" trademark serial number 73536336, the "Jumpman" trademark serial number 77276692, and the actual Jumpman logo serial numbers 74000758 and 73728115. Yes, Michael is the one who inspired the image of the trademark and made the Air Jordan brand the most sought-after brand for shoes and apparel, but Michael doesn't own the rights to the Jumpman logo or the Air Jordan mark.

Michael seems to be ok with whatever deal he has with Nike, so no judgment. Even if Michael is satisfied with the agreement, he has in place with Nike, if a dispute between

Michael and Nike occurred over the brand, Nike would likely prevail as the rightful owner of the trademark and copyright. As an athlete or entertainer, you could work to establish a brand and lose it all if you don't own it, or at least jointly own it. Therefore, you should highly consider maintaining ownership over your brand. Maybe if some people knew the potential value of their mark and how to protect it before entering into a business dealing, like you are learning now, their situations would have been different.

Sharing a Band Brand

An artist's brand can be a stage name, a band name, or some other type of identifier that qualifies as a trademark. It is not just athletes and business owners who should focus on trademarking their brand for heightened protection. Entertainers are providing a service under a brand, so they should do so as well.

The Street Code encourages entertainers to focus on being a performer rather than thinking about operating as a business. A lot of times, people other than the entertainer – managers, accountants, associates, record labels – handle the entertainer's personal and professional business. These hired individuals may be the ones in control of legal issues such as intellectual property protection, including the trademarking and protection of trademarks.

There have been entertainers who allowed these individuals to handle their business and were surprised to learn that the name on the "owner" line of the trademark registration was not the entertainer themselves. If you don't involve yourself in your process, you could find yourself investing time, talent, and money into a brand that someone on your "team" claims you gave ownership to and the right to control.

The entertainer, like the athlete, will benefit from thinking of what they do as a business. There should be a level of understanding between the entertainer and his or her management team of the importance of protecting the entertainer's name or likeness. They should also understand the consequence of not doing so. The entertainer may lose rights to what they built for lack of understanding. Losing these rights and protection may result in the entertainer's inability to use their own name and likeness.

Claiming rightful ownership of a brand intensifies with artists in bands. Generally, each artist will share ownership in a trademark with the other band members unless they agree otherwise. Band members usually don't establish or layout the details of how to manage crucial decisions related to the ownership of the band's trademark in the beginning. Under the Street Code, it is ok to forego discussing the serious details and to not think about what can go wrong in the future. It's easier and "less businessy" to focus on how right things are going now because that's how it will always be. Well, if things do not go as planned, the result may look like the catfight in *Brother Records, Inc. (Plaintiff) v. Jardine (Defendant)* case.

In 1961, Al Jardine, Mike Love, Brian Wilson, Carl Wilson, and Dennis Wilson formed The Beach Boys. The band achieved substantial commercial success. They produced numerous hit songs and toured to huge audiences throughout the country. In 1967, the members of The Beach Boys incorporated Brother Records, Inc. (BRI) to hold and administer the intellectual property rights for "The Beach Boys." Accordingly, BRI became the registered owner of the "The Beach Boys" trademark. In the 1980s, the band's original members dismantled. Carl Wilson had died, Mike Love and Al Jardine no longer wanted to tour together, and Brian Wilson did not want to tour at all. At that time, Al Jardine, Mike Love, Brian Wilson, and the estate of Carl Wilson were all equal owners of BRI as shareholders and directors.

Al wanted to tour solo and still use The Beach Boys name. The BRI directors agreed to license the use of the trademark to anyone who wanted to continue to use the group's name. One of the stipulations was that the licensee had to use a booking agent and manager from an approved list in the license agreement. Al agreed to the license and signed it, but BRI wanted other assurances and would not sign the license agreement until those assurances were received.

In the beginning, Al and his band continued to perform under the terms of the license agreement using names that included 'The Beach Boys' trademark. At one point, Al's attorney sent BRI a letter stating that Al and his band would be performing as "Beach Boys Family and Friends. Therefore, a license from BRI [was] unnecessary." On October 28, 1998, BRI told Al that his unlicensed use of the trademark was an infringement. Subsequently, BRI filed an infringement claim, and the court granted summary judgment in favor of BRI.

In *Brother Records, Inc. v. Jardine,* the dispute was based on one band member not wanting to be held hostage by the other four. I'm sure things were great when they started, and the band members were fine with operating under the Street Code at that time. However, it wasn't until they dismantled and wanted to do their own thing with the brand that they all helped bring to commercial success, that they began to think about creating an agreement on how to license the band's trademark. Trying to figure out the details on how each member could use the trademark at a time when things were no longer going right, landed them in court. Forming an agreement on the use of "The Beach Boys" trademark before they attained their commercial success would have been the thing to do under the Legal Code!

The next case involves a band and one bandmember's change of heart. In *Robert C. Kaufhold and Joseph Arthur McGukin (Plaintiffs) v. Cyclopian Music, Inc. and Gerald Caiafa (Defendants)*, all it took was for one bandmember to break the "handshake will do" mentality of the Street Code to land them in court. As this case will show, whoever breaks from the Street Code to operate under the Legal Code first may have the upper hand.

Robert and Joseph are two former members of the band "Misfits." Joseph was the band's longest-serving drummer playing from 1979 to 1982. Robert was the band's guitarist from 1978 to 1980. Gerald, known under the pseudonym "Jerry Only," was the band's bass guitarist and one of the band's original members since the formation of the group in 1977. Robert and Joseph sued Gerald's music label Cyclopian Music, Inc. seeking a declaratory judgment from the court, alleging that they were co-owners of the Misfits trademarks based on a settlement agreement reached in a prior lawsuit. Robert and Joseph were not a part of the conversation for that agreement.

Robert and Joseph alleged that Gerald told them about the settlement agreement regarding ownership of the "Misfit Marks" that was executed between Gerald and the other former band members. The agreement stated that each of the former members of the band (including them), and parties to the settlement agreement, co-owned various Misfits Marks, including the "Misfits" name and imagery, and no member would apply for exclusive rights to use the Misfits Marks.

Based on this communication, Robert and Joseph believed that Gerald would not seek to gain exclusive control over the Misfits Marks. Conversely, Gerald and his music label Cyclopian filed five applications with the USPTO to register the Misfits Marks. Three of those applications matured into trademark registrations. Gerald represented in court that Cyclopian owned the Misfits Marks and that to the best of his knowledge and belief, no other person had the right to use the marks in commerce.

Robert and Joseph stated in the lawsuit that they contributed their talents, money, time, and resources to develop the band's image and brand. Gerald's band used the Misfit logos and stylized versions of the name to identify itself. Gerald's band toured using the Misfits name and performed songs from the old catalog in addition to new music that was released periodically since 1997. Although Robert and Joseph ceased performing with the band in the early 1980s, sales from recordings on which they performed continued to generate royalties. They collected these royalties until right before the case was filed. Robert and Joseph relied on an alleged verbal communication with Gerald regarding what the settlement, which they never laid eyes on, said about co-ownership. They should have requested a copy of the settlement or had something putting in writing after the conversation with Gerald took place, but they did not.

Although there may have been a verbal understanding between the various members of the band under the Street Code, Gerald followed the Legal Code by registering the Misfit Marks. The court granted Gerald's motion to dismiss the suit against him and Robert and Joseph's claim of co-ownership of the Misfit Marks.

Pussycat Copycat

As mentioned earlier, trademark infringement happens in the film industry as well. One of the landmark cases that set a precedent on this type of violation in the film industry is *Dallas Cowboys Cheerleaders Inc. v. Pussycat Cinema Ltd.* Dallas Cowboys Cheerleaders brought a suit against the film production company for using an imitation of their trademark. In the film, the production company used uniforms, color combinations, and other symbols that were similar to that of the Dallas Cowboys Cheerleaders. The production company presented ads with captions such as "starring ex-Dallas cowgirl cheerleaders." In viewing the facts of this case, the court found that Dallas Cowboys Cheerleaders was successful in their argument against Pussycat Cinema.

Remember the discussion in the History section laying out the evolution of trademark protection. Trademark protection started with a particularly narrow focus, which, over time, expanded to protecting trademarks from being exploited in any manner that could confuse the public into believing there was an affiliation with the rightful owner. This case was an example of capitalizing on a protected brand by claiming affiliation, even though the actual brand and trademark were not directly used. Creation of knock off advertisements or knock-off products can take you down a slippery slope, don't find yourself involved in providing or creating knock offs that could be determined to be infringing on an established and protected brand.

As a Matter of Law

I discussed fair use as a defense in the Copyright section. Fair use is also a defense argument raised when an individual has been accused of unauthorized use of someone else's trademark. While the fair use analysis is different under trademark law, and the copyright four-factor test does not apply, the outcome is just as unpredictable.

In *Timelines, Inc., (Plaintiff) v. Facebook, Inc. (Defendant)*, Facebook asserted the affirmative defense of fair use. Timelines filed a complaint against Facebook, alleging four counts of federal and state trademark claims. The court required Facebook to prove three elements to assert a successful fair use defense, (1) it did not use the mark as a trademark; (2) the use was in a descriptive sense; and (3) the use was made in good faith. To begin its analysis, the court elaborated on the five categories identifying the strength of a mark and the protections that follow. The more distinctive the mark, the stronger the protections will be. The court started its discussion by pointing out a registered trademark is entitled to the presumption of validity. Meaning, a registered trademark is presumed not to be "merely descriptive" or generic. If the trademark is descriptive, it must have acquired a secondary meaning related to the owner. Facebook had to rebut this presumption and prove that the mark was generic or descriptive, and if the trademark was descriptive, there was no established secondary meaning.

Through the Timelines website, Timelines.com, a user can record the details of events and connect these events in space and through time to other related activities. The linking of events in this way contributes to a better collective understanding of what occurred at a particular place and time. Timeline owns the federal trademark registrations for Timelines, Timelines.com, and the "Timelines" design mark and uses these registered marks in connection with its goods and services.

Facebook included a "Timeline" feature on Facebook. com. The feature consists of a summary of a user's life since birth by using updates made to a user's profile on the website. Facebook featured "Timeline" as a product. The court found Facebook had marketed the feature in a manner that a reasonable jury might find it to be trademark use. Therefore, the first element of fair use weighed against Facebook.

The court further found that Timelines' trademarks weren't considered generic or descriptive without meaning. Instead, Timelines' trademarks were strong marks that represented the Timelines' brand in the consumers' minds. Therefore, the second factor of the fair use analysis weighed against Facebook. The court reasoned, Facebook used the mark in such a manner that the consumer could be misled to believe Facebook was connected in some way to Timeline, or Facebook was the new owner of the mark.

Facebook knew of Timeline and the services it offered. They even knew of some users believing there was a connection. This knowledge resulted in the third and final factor weighing against Facebook. Facebook acted under the Street Code mentality when it created a duplicate of a protected brand under the pretense of fair use. However, they failed to demonstrate as a matter of law under the Legal Code that the use of the Timelines' marks was actually fair, and therefore, the court denied Facebook summary judgment.

CONCLUSION

"Yesterday I was clever, so I wanted to change the world.
Today I am wise, so I am changing myself."
-Rumi

Protecting your brand through trademarking is a process that starts with choosing a strong mark, registering it, promoting it, and policing it. A trademark is a connection between you and your company and can be the most valuable asset your company owns. Protecting your trademark can be achieved through common law, state registration, or federal registration. A federally registered trademark identifies you as the source of your product or service nationally. Trademark infringement occurs when a person tries to sell a product or service using an identical or similar mark that exists. Infringement can happen unknowingly for the lack of research, or knowingly to take advantage of the goodwill customers have associated with another brand. Infringing on a trademark can have legal implications that can range from receiving cease and desist letters to being served a legal complaint in a lawsuit.

Remember, you are a business. No matter what industry you are in, if you are providing a service or product to consumers, you run a business. You should make serious efforts to research and create a mark that represents your brand. The Street Code will have you focus on marketing and promotion in the earlier stages, with little to no thought about making sure your business is legally sound. If you choose a mark that you later discover is not federally registerable and legally protectable, you may find yourself contemplating the need to start all over. Or, you may find yourself stuck operating under limited protection after putting all your effort into marketing and promoting a brand that you can't federally protect.

You want to seek the highest level of protection for your brand that you can. Although registration is voluntary, you should ask yourself, are you fine with being limited to a geographical area? Are you willing to co-exist with a similar brand?

Take the initiative to understand the trademark process. If you are an athlete or entertainer, don't leave the management of your brand in other people's hands. Have some involvement in your business. Ask questions and request a copy of the paperwork. Hire a trademark attorney who will have your best interest in mind. Having legal guidance in this legal proceeding can help tremendously. Or, you can take the initiative and do your due diligence in learning the USPTO requirements and process. Trademark registration can be a very nuanced proceeding.

Don't lose money trying to figure it out when there are professionals that can help you.

Two things to keep in mind: Don't infringe on other people's marks and do everything possible to protect yours.

CODE V. CODE
RIGHT TO PRIVACY

Street Code v. Legal Code

United States (2020)

FACTS

> *"People often claim to hunger for truth,*
> *but seldom like the taste when it's served up."*
> **-George R.R. Martin**

A Civil Tort

A tort is a civil violation made upon an individual. Violating the right to privacy is a tort that provides legal recourse to a person that has been harmed. While every person should expect to have a right to control their privacy, certain circumstances may affect that right. It is crucial to understand when those rights are affected, and when they are not.

The Constitution and Bill of Rights give implied protection to the right to privacy. State and federal law provide an expressed protection to the right to privacy. There are four activities prohibited under the right to privacy law: <u>Intrusion on Seclusion</u>, <u>Appropriation</u>, <u>Public Disclosure of Private Facts</u>, and <u>False Light</u>. The right to privacy law is essential for an athlete, entertainer, and entrepreneur to understand. Knowing the protections and prohibitions provided by the Legal Code will help preserve rights and assist you in avoiding a violation of someone else's rights. For this guide, our focus will be specifically on appropriation, which a prohibited tort under common law and the right to privacy law. Violating the privacy of individuals happens quite often in the sports, entertainment, and business industries. Athletes and entertainers will generally find themselves on the side of being violated, and businesses frequently find themselves on the side of violating.

Name Image and Likeness

Rights to privacy can be broken down into two types of violations in most states. Violation of privacy rights can be viewed under the common law tort of appropriation (misappropriation) or under the codified state law tort (right of publicity). Although the rights are generally merged into one, gaining a general understanding of how both are applied differently in an alleged violation is beneficial. Courts do handle them slightly differently. To give you a general sense, here is a summary of the differences. We will go deeper into the different elements required for each of these invasions of privacy in the Rules section of this guide.

Misappropriation under common law generally applies to the unwanted or unauthorized use of the likeness of an ordinary person. A court may find that by violating a person's right to privacy, a benefit was realized with or without a commercial gain. The harm under this invasion is the mere fact the individual's personal privacy was violated.

The right of publicity tort, on the other hand, generally applies to any unauthorized use of a celebrity name or identity. There is usually commercial gain as a result of invading the celebrity's personal privacy and property. The harm under this invasion is that the use of the celebrity's likeness is an invasion of their property rights and commercial value.

The scope of protection afforded by the right of publicity varies widely from state to state. For example, one state may protect against the use of a name, image, and likeness. Another state may add voice and sound to the list of protections. It may be a good time to point out that a corporation cannot invoke the right to privacy. The right to privacy protection is for individuals. In other words, an entrepreneur cannot raise an invasion of privacy claim if someone impedes on their company brand. Instead, they would need to protect the company brand under other laws, including trademark, copyright, or unfair competition, but not right to privacy laws.

Notorious Issue

A typical invasion of privacy rights in sports and entertainment is the unauthorized use of athlete's and entertainer's images. In business, the issue arises when an entrepreneur uses the image or likeness of any ordinary person or celebrity for commercial gain without permission or if they have permission, and the use goes beyond the scope of the consent given.

The Street Code lends itself to this notorious belief that a person's image or likeness is fair game. Under the Street Code, the use of a picture, video, recording, and the like, to promote products, events, services, sell stories, will be done without obtaining permission if the image is accessible. In my experience, this commonly happens in film projects, the selling of merchandise, and the promotion of entertainment events.

HISTORY

*"We aren't in an information age;
we are in an entertainment age."*
-Tony Robbins

Setting Boundaries

Maintaining the right to privacy is essential, and it is taken for granted more often than it should be. Privacy is a relatively young concept in law, and a complex theory for the general public. The idea of the right to be free from an invasion of privacy under a tort law was born from an article written by Samuel Warren and Louis Brandeis entitled *-The Right to Privacy*, 4 Harvard L.R. 193 (1890). "Privacy" is defined in this article as the right to be left alone. The article addressed how technology had changed individual privacy in the photography industry. In the past, photographers needed a cooperative subject who sat still for a prolonged period of time to allow the proper exposure to capture the image. New technology, however, was going to allow for quick, sly snapshots of subjects. Samuel and Louis seemed to foresee the issues that continuing technological advancement was going to present. In their prediction, they knew there was going to be a need to start a conversation about setting boundaries when it came to privacy. This foresight necessitated the recognition of the tort-based right to privacy.

In the sports and entertainment industry, the Street Code established this notion that losing privacy was a price you had to pay with fame. The rise of social media pushed this mentality in a way such that invading one's privacy was not an issue only experienced by the famous it became a private citizen issue as well. Samuel and Louis were correct in their predictions that there was going to be a need to start looking at privacy as a protected right under the Legal Code.

It wasn't until 50 years after the publication of *The Right to Privacy* that the legal system codified the privacy laws in what is called the Restatement of Torts. In 1953, the case *Haelan Laboratories, Inc. v. Topps Chewing Gum, Inc.* established a distinction between the invasion of the right to privacy versus the right of publicity. Let me help you understand what distinctions evolved, and what you should be considering, by looking at the next two cases. I will expound on the differences in more depth in the Rules section.

Portrayed as Endorsing

Advertisements have been the cause of many claims against businesses for the invasion of privacy rights of another. Business owners, especially small business owners, regularly take chances and use images and likenesses of individuals without permission for advertising. If you are a small business owner, you may have, at one time or another, considered doing the same to save on the cost of creating original images or paying professionals (models, celebrities, photographers). But you could run the risk of violating a privacy right of the person portrayed if you take that route. Digitally altering photos for personal use or using the likeness of an individual beyond the scope of the permission given can be an entrepreneur's mousetrap. One of the earliest misappropriation claims for endorsements was in *Paolo Pavesich v. New England Life Insurance Co.*

In this 1905 case, Paolo's image was used in a newspaper advertisement for life insurance. The photo in the ad portrayed the fictional sentiment that he was glad he purchased insurance during the "healthy and productive period" of his life. The Georgia Supreme Court moved forward with a cause of action for misappropriation of Paolo's image. The court ruled in his favor. The court noted, "the publication of one's picture without his consent by another, as an advertisement, for the mere purpose of increasing the profits and other gains of the advertiser" is misappropriation. The court held that the right not to be portrayed as endorsing a commercial enterprise applies regardless of whether the person actually uses or recommends that product.

In this case, Paolo was not a celebrity. He was a private citizen who had his likeness used by a business to promote their insurance. The use of his image by a company without permission was a violation of his personal rights. Now let's move from a private citizen violation to the unauthorized use of a celebrity's likeness.

The 1953 *Haelan Laboratories, Inc. v. Topps Chewing Gum, Inc.* case involved the commercial use of an athlete's likeness. This case involved rival manufacturers of chewing gum, both of whom packaged baseball cards with their gum as a sales promotion. Haelan had exclusive contracts with several baseball players who waived their right to privacy claims related to the use of their names and likenesses on the baseball cards.

One of the baseball players entered into a contract with rival manufacturer Topps Chewing Gum. Haelan filed a claim with the Second Circuit alleging inducement of breach of contract when the rival manufacturer used the baseball player's image. The court, however, decided not to analyze this issue as a breach of contract. Instead, the court focused on the right to privacy analysis from a commercial standpoint. It looked at the baseball player's agreement with Haelan and the terms in the contract prohibiting the baseball player from using his image. In making their ruling, the court held that independent of any right to privacy, "a man has a right in the publicity value of his photograph." In other words, they were stating that a person has a right to their own image. The court continued, "as a result of this right, as long as the defendant didn't induce the breach, there will be no liability." In other words, a major league baseball player has a recognizable property right in the publicity value of his photograph.

The holding, in this case, set a precedent on raising an invasion of privacy claim with a focus on "rights of publicity." This ruling is credited as the first case to establish the right of publicity doctrine by extending proprietary protection to a celebrity's right to privacy (different from Paolo's situation as a private citizen) and also giving the celebrity the ability to make a profit off their own likeness.

Merch

Privacy violations occur quite often with the selling of merchandise, "merch," with the unauthorized use of a person's name, likeness, or other forms of identity. Merch provides the means of displaying cultural affinity through its message-carrying capacity. Consumers generally buy merch because of what it symbolizes. Slapping someone's image on a t-shirt, hat, cup, or other paraphernalia before seeking permission is standard practice under the Street Code. Whether the person is well-known or not, using an individual's likeness to sell a product or promote a message is not permitted without obtaining express permission, especially if there is a monetary benefit sought by using someone else's property. When creating or selling merch, the Street Code reinforces the notion that privacy is elusive and profit is exclusive. Meaning that in the mind of the infringer, privacy is a fair game, but the profits earned of exploiting someone are not.

The takeaway? As the Legal Code continues to evolve in this area of law, there is a need to rethink the differences between misappropriation and right of publicity. The consequences of improper use and the requirements for protection under the Legal Code are slightly different in each area of law. In the Application section, we will look at issues that the Street Code mentality has created for the individuals selling merch. As well as for the individuals who have had their privacy rights violated. Hopefully, this will help you if you find yourself on either end of the issue.

ISSUE

"I do not regard advertising as entertainment or an art form, but as a medium of information."
-David Ogilvy

Notable Figures

The are several issues to address in the area of the right to privacy. Generally, questions come from both sides of the spectrum. There are questions raised by entities wanting to use the likeness of an individual. There are also questions raised by individuals whose likeness has, or could be, used by others.

In the context of the entertainment and sports industries, questions tend to arise around whether it is permissible for a person to use a notable entertainer or athlete's likeness to promote an event or sell merch. These questions are raised by small business owners as well as from less notable athletes and entertainers. Usually, they want to use the more celebrated athletes or entertainers' likeness to promote or gain more exposure for their services in the industry.

The Street Code suggests that if the image was shared online, it must be fair game. With social media and online access, people regularly download images for personal use and many times commercial use. An entertainer may create a promotional flyer for a party and use a notable artist's picture on the flyer that was copied and pasted from a website. An individual may promote a sports camp and use a notable athlete's picture from a social media site on their marketing material or t-shirts

Deceased Public Figure

What if the person is deceased? Is it permissible to use the image and likeness of notable figures that are deceased? We see Marilyn Monroe, Bob Marley, Elvis Presley, Michael Jackson, Prince, and so on, printed on many t-shirts. Is everyone who prints merch with these celebrity images seeking express permission? Does everyone have to? There are exceptions to the Legal Code, but the exceptions are very specific and very limited. You need to know if your use fits into any exception. If not, you could find yourself in a Street Code v. Legal Code battle. If not now, it could happen later.

Beyond the Scope

With the uptick in podcasts and vlogs, questions arise surrounding media entrepreneurs and the use of images and likenesses of those interviewed. If you are a new podcaster, or you have been doing it for a while, you need to ask and answer the following question. If a person agrees to give an interview or appear on a podcast, is it permissible to use the image and likeness of that individual beyond the scope of the initial meeting?

The Application section of this guide addresses these questions and their answers. I present legal cases where these issues arose, and the court provided a clear opinion under the Legal Code.

RULES

"If they come for me in the morning,
they will come for you in the night."
-Angela Davis

Private Citizen, Public Celebrity

The general, privacy law for appropriation prohibits the unauthorized use of someone's name, likeness, or form of his or her identity. This protection applies to both private citizens and public figures under the tort of privacy law. Specifically, laws against misappropriation seek to protect the personal interest of a person's privacy.

Generally, a private citizen would file a misappropriation claim stating invasion of privacy. This type of complaint involves the unwanted and unauthorized use of the name or likeness of an ordinary person. The misappropriation could apply to images used for business advertising or other such commercial purposes. The general rule for private citizen claims is that the individual does not have to prove the commercial value of the image or likeness to prevail. That is why a non-celebrity usually raises this claim. An infringer could still be held liable for any non-commercial use if the person's identity is exploited for an infringer's benefit. The injury claimed from this violation can be justified by mental anguish or embarrassment that may result or if there was any financial gain received by the infringer.

The right of publicity involves the appropriation of a celebrity's name or identity for commercial purposes only. The Legal Code embedded in the right of publicity seeks to protect the property interest that a celebrity has in their name, image, or likeness. Therefore, the injury sought under this violation usually results from an economic interference more than it does from an embarrassment or mental anguish. There must be some commercial interest or market value usurped when claiming there has been right of publicity violation to use a celebrity likeness.

In some states, celebrities can't even sue for invasion of privacy under misappropriation of name and likeness; a claim has to be under the right of publicity. This is based on the thought that celebrities have no privacy interest to protect when it comes to the use of their celebrity. However, they do have an economic right to protect when it comes to the use of their celebrity. Likewise, noncelebrities generally may not sue for violation of the right of publicity based on the thought that the use of the likeness of ordinary, uncelebrated people has no commercial value. However, it is becoming more common for states to permit celebrities and non-celebrities alike to sue under either, or both, of these stated claims if they can establish the appropriate harm.

Right to Privacy vs. Right of Publicity

The following two cases address the differences between claims of right to privacy (misappropriation) and right of publicity and how the court applies the Legal Code based on the type of complaint filed.

In this case, *Charles Ainsworth (Plaintiff) v. Century Supply Co. (Defendant),* Century hired Charles to install tile at the house of its sales manager. Charles agreed that Century could record him installing the flooring for the limited purposes of sharing the video with Century's customers as an instructional guide. However, Century used the footage beyond the scope of permission granted when it used the video in commercials. Charles sued the company for "invasion of privacy by appropriating his likeness."

Initially, Charles filed a claim for "infringement to his right of publicity" but dropped that claim before moving forward. By removing the right of publicity claim, Charles did not have to prove he had commercial value in the use of his likeness to make a persuasive argument to the court to achieve a successful outcome. He only had to show mental anguish brought about by the unauthorized use of the video, and that the use of his likeness served to benefit the company.

The court granted him a monetary award even though he could not prove he possessed a commercial value in his likeness as a celebrity would have. The court noted that the monetary judgment awarded was to uphold Charles's rights against Century's unauthorized use based on his argument that the impermissible use upset him and caused his mental anguish.

Charles more than likely did not have to drop his right of publicity claim. However, he may not have prevailed on that issue if he had failed to prove the commercial value of using his likeness. By focusing on a misappropriation complaint, he was able to concentrate on the fact that the unauthorized use of the video caused him mental anguish; therefore, his rights as an ordinary individual were violated.

Let's compare the facts of Charles's case to the following situation.

In *People for the Ethical Treatment of Animals- PETA (Appellant) v. Bobby Bersoni (Respondent)*, Bobby filed a counterclaim for misappropriation of his likeness by PETA. The misappropriation claim was the same as Charles' claim in his complaint, but the court's ruling was different.

In this case, Bobby was a famous world-renowned animal trainer. Someone filmed him shaking, punching, and hitting his trained orangutans backstage. The footage was shared with PETA, who then used the video on their platform and shared it publicly. Bobby filed suit for invasion of privacy, misappropriating his likeness through the dissemination of the recorded video of him with his animals. Bobby expressed to the court that he did not experience any mental anguish from the sharing of the video; he had an issue with PETA profiting of his celebrity. Bobby argued in his counterclaim that he was looking to recover on the economic gain acquired by PETA for using the video. The court held that Bobby could not prevail on his argument based on the type of claim he filed. A misappropriation claim is used to recover damages for mental anguish, which he denied he had experienced. Bobby was unsuccessful in his counterclaim because he admitted that he did not experience mental anguish over the sharing of the filmed video. If he had suffered an embarrassment or mental distress or contended that he had done so, he could have prevailed under the claim of misappropriation. Instead, he argued he sought damages for commercial gain of his celebrity status.

With celebrity status, Bobby could have filed for violation of the right of publicity in addition to his misappropriation claim. By filing a right of publicity claim, he may have had a different outcome and been awarded damages based on PETA's economic, or business, gain for publicly sharing the video with him in it.

State Court

To reiterate one more time, an invasion of privacy misappropriation is generally an issue with a violation of the rights of privacy for a private citizen. A right of publicity infringement is a type of "persona" rights claim. Both causes of action can be pursued in state court. Proving an invasion of the right to privacy or right to publicity claim varies from state to state. Some states have some form of right of publicity statute, while others do not. Having a statute is not a prerequisite for the right of publicity to be enforceable in any given jurisdiction. With or without a publicity statute on the books, many states will arrive at the same outcome by analyzing the Legal Code under common law invasion of privacy through appropriation. Since the laws are different from state to state, knowing how your state prohibits or permits the use of another's likeness is something that you should find out if you're an entrepreneur or in the sports or entertainment industries.

In Georgia, for example, the right of publicity protection is the right to the exclusive use of an individual's name and likeness. Liability arises when unauthorized use of a person's name or likeness is made for "financial gain." Also, the law prohibits invasion of privacy on one's rights by misappropriating their likeness without permission in an advertisement. This prohibition does not require proving the commercial value of a person's name or likeness or require there was a "financial gain" of unauthorized use.

Defenses

Three defenses can be raised against a claim for appropriating an individual's likeness: consent, First Amendment protections, and the statute of limitations.

Consent is an absolute defense of invasion of privacy misappropriation claims. Meaning consent is your most sound defense. When you gather information or take photographs of an individual, it is a good practice to ask for consent to use the photos or information in the manner you intend. You should consider all the ways you intend to use an individual likeness and get consent for each intention. You should take this approach to obtain consent whether the content is to be used for a website, blog, vlog, or other online platforms. It is best to have this permission in writing whenever possible.

The First Amendment protections are included in the U.S. Bill of Rights to protect free expression. The First Amendment grants an exception on the use of an individual name, image, or likeness if it is for news and commentary. As such, there are some limitations on claiming an invasion of privacy under appropriation. If the actual use is not related to the news or commentary presented, the exception may not apply. Furthermore, if the news or commentary reported shows more than what is necessary to convey a general message or the "report" covers a celebrity's entire performance in a broadcast, the exception may not apply.

The First Amendment also protects creative works. This protection includes, but is not limited to, novels that mention real-life figures, historical fiction, movies based loosely on real-life events, docudramas, and acts of parody directed at an individual. State courts look at the creative or artistic work in question on a case-by-case basis to determine if the First Amendment protection outweighs the right to privacy of the private citizen or celebrity.

Finally, the statute of limitations applies to the amount of time an individual has to file a lawsuit and may also be used as a defense. State law sets a time limit to file a complaint from the date of the alleged violation, the date of first publication, or exhibition of the offending use of the individual's or celebrity's name or likeness. The amount of time varies from state to state and can be anywhere from one to six years after the alleged violation. In the Application section, we will see how this rule is applied in case law.

APPLICATION

"You are your best thing."
- *Toni Morrison*

Speech With a Cost

The Legal Code protects citizens' rights to free speech under the First Amendment by extending the defense of free speech to what otherwise would be a violation under the invasion of privacy appropriation tort. The Legal Code also puts limitations on how the First Amendment can be raised as a defense.

Free speech is not so free when it is entangled in elements that are not protected. Whether the expression involves a celebrity or a private citizen, it is crucial to understand what is prohibited and permitted.

Although celebrities have limited protection of privacy compared to that of private citizens, they do have expanded protections of property interest and impermissible economic interference. It's best to err on the side of caution and keep in mind all speech is not free speech contrary to Street Code beliefs. Your speech may come at a price if you violate the First Amendment exceptions or receive a benefit or attain some type of financial gain from how you exploit an individual's image or likeness.

Case by Case, Court by Court

The next case illustrates how the analysis of free speech can differ based on the judge or jury analyzing the facts of the case. In *Michael Jordan (Plaintiff) v. Jewel Food Stores, Inc. (Defendant)*, two courts interpreted the use of Michael Jordan's image from different perspectives under the protections provided by the First Amendment. In 2009, Michael was inducted into the Naismith Memorial Basketball Hall of Fame. Time magazine printed a "Sports Illustrated Presents" commemorative issue celebrating Michael's career and desired to publish an advertisement ("ad") that referenced Michael Jordan. The magazine solicited several businesses to design a one-page ad for the issue. They suggested that there be some sort of play on words or design, but the ad should mainly highlight Michael Jordan. Jewel was one of the businesses solicited and accepted Time magazine's request.

The drugstore designed an ad featuring an image of a pair of sneakers with the number "23." The ad mentioned Michael's name and identified the drugstore by its name, stylized logo, and slogan. Michael sued under the state privacy protection for violation of the right of publicity.

Despite the ad's reference to Michael's identity, the district court deemed the speech was a congratulatory message. This court viewed the ad as non-commercial and held that although the nature of the business is economically motivated, the ad did not solicit anyone, did not request viewers to buy anything, and did not promote a specific product or service that the drugstore sold. Accordingly, the court concluded the advertisement was not commercial speech and was protected under the First Amendment.

Under appeal, the Seventh Circuit held to the contrary. This court noted that although Jewel's ad did not promote or sell a specific product or service, its purpose as "image advertising" was enough to classify the ad as commercial speech. As a result, the court of appeals barred Jewel's First Amendment non-commercial speech defense. The court's decision focused on the context of the ad, which included Jewel's graphic logo and slogan. The court found that including the logo and slogan into the Michael Jordan ad promoted the store and therefore had an economic motivation behind creating the ad to encourage consumers to shop at the store.

The court reasoned that "modern advertising is highly creative. The consumer does not have to be invited to purchase a specific product for an advertisement to be deemed commercial speech." Jewel's advertisement served two functions: (1) congratulating Michael and (2) enhancing Jewel's brand. The ad accomplished this by associating itself with Michael in the minds of basketball fans and Chicago consumers. Finding in favor of Michael, the advertisement was not protected, and Jewel was liable for the damages sought by the plaintiff.

Pre-existing Commercial Value

The Street Code suggests that if a person is not famous, they should be happy to get some sort of recognition. The thought is, no harm, no foul because the privacy of the ordinary, non-celebrated individual has no value anyway. Entrepreneurs or small business owners sometimes target non-celebrated individuals for promotional advertisements or marketing materials related to a product or service to reduce costs or simply because they are more accessible. Neither of these reasons excludes the fact the Legal Code declares that the use of an individual's image or likeness without permission may be a violation of their right to privacy.

If someone uses your image or something affiliated with your identity, you can demand compensation for the use of your image or demand that your image not be used unless the user can prevail on one of the defenses discussed in the Rules section of this guide. Remember, don't consent to have someone use your image or likeness because consent is an absolute defense against you. Even if consent was given for one type of use, that doesn't mean you lose total control of how your image or likeness is used in other contexts.

This applies to individuals seeking to use someone else's likeness as well. Defenses to allegations of invasion of the privacy of a private citizen are looked at more stringently than those applied to celebrities. Regardless, keep in mind that if you are the person utilizing another's likeness and you cannot defend your actions, your business could be damaged or jeopardized.

Let me share some more cases on the right to privacy of a private citizen that addresses the issues of commercial value and the scope of consent.

In *Lindsay Bullard (Plaintiff) v. Joe Francis and MRA Holding, LLC,* the court addressed both the issue of commercial value and scope of consent. Entrepreneur Joe Francis created the "Girls Gone Wild" series featuring young and sometimes underage women, who at times, performed explicit sex acts either with partial or total nudity. Lindsay exposed her breasts to two unknown men in a parking lot in Panama City, Florida. She was aware at the time that the men were videotaping her and made no objection. Lindsay did not inquire how the men might use the videotape at the time. MRA Holding obtained possession of the recording and included the footage in its College Girls Gone Wild video series.

MRA Holding also used a still shot image of Lindsay captured from the video. The image was placed on the cover of the College Girls Gone Wild video with the words "Get Educated!" across her breast. The inscription arguably indicated that Lindsay was encouraging others to "Get Educated!" by purchasing the video. Lindsay looks to be endorsing the College Girls Gone Wild video with her image on the cover.

The court exclaimed that MRA's use of the image suggested it was part of an advertisement. The defendants argued that Lindsay's image and likeness didn't have commercial value that would give rise to a legal claim and that she consented to the recording because she knew that they were recording her and did not object.

The court made it clear that consenting to the recording of the video is not equivalent to agreeing to have one's picture placed on the cover of the packaging of a commercially distributed videotape. As for the need for Lindsay's likeness to have commercial value, the court remarked that it had previously stated the interest protected in an appropriation case is the plaintiff's exclusive right to protect his or her name and likeness. Safeguarding is an inherent aspect of his [or her] identity with or without possessing a commercial value. In this case, the court found no conflict between Lindsay's right to privacy and MRA's freedoms of speech and press. Thus, Lindsay prevailed in her right to privacy appropriation claim.

This case was tried in Georgia. Georgia law does not require a private citizen to have any inherent or preexisting commercial value to maintain a viable claim to their rights to privacy and protection from having their name and photograph used without consent for financial gain. Furthermore, giving consent for a specific use does not mean consent was given for any and every use. Keep in mind, a slight change in the facts could make a difference in how consent is viewed. The next case involves the same defendants under similar circumstances with a different outcome.

Voluntarily Participated

We have discussed consent as a defense to the use of a person's image and likeness. As you saw in the previous case, Lindsay voluntarily participated in being recorded in a video. However, her participation in the video did not mean that she gave consent to have her still image used on the cover to promote the video. If Lindsay's claim related solely to the objection of being in the video itself, the outcome may have been different. The use of the cover image in the manner presented went beyond the scope of her explicit or implied consent. The next case addresses what a court may look at to determine if consent does apply to the use of a private citizen's likeness, even if they object.

The *Veronica Lane (Plaintiff) v. MRA Holdings, LLC.* (Defendant) allows us to compare the factors of consent to Lindsay's case. This lawsuit involved the same Girl's Gone Wild series, but this time the case was tried in the

Middle District of Florida. Although this claim didn't fall under the Georgia jurisdiction like the previous case, Florida law was based on the same premise. The court analyzed whether section 540.08 of the Florida code was violated by MRA's display of Veronica exposing her breasts in a "Girls Gone Wild" video. Just like Lindsay, Veronica consented to be videotaped but was unaware that the video would go public and be sold.

The purpose of section 540.08 of the Florida code is to prevent the use of a person's name or likeness to directly promote a product or service. Under the Florida statute, the terms "trade," "commercial," or "advertising purpose" refer to the direct promotion of a product or service. Therefore, the way that the user associates the person's name or personality with a product or service is a determining factor in finding direct promotion exists.

The court found it irrefutable that the Girls Gone Wild video was an expressive work created solely for entertainment purposes. The court also found it indisputable that while Veronica's image and likeness were used to sell copies of Girls Gone Wild, her image and likeness were never associated with a product or service unrelated to that expressive work. MRA never presented her as endorsing or promoting a product or message about their product. Rather, how they portrayed Veronica was seen as part of an expressive work in which she voluntarily participated. As a matter of section 540.08, the court held that Veronica's image and likeness were not used to promote a product or service for "trade" or a "commercial" or "advertising purpose." The court ruled in favor of MRA in this action.

Personae on Merch

The Street Code would have you believe that if an individual is deceased, the use of their image or likeness is permissible. The Legal Code says this is not the case. Like most other laws, each state has specific requirements related to protections afforded to a deceased public figure.

You know that it is important to seek permission to use the likeness of public figures that are living, and if you didn't, you know now. But it is also necessary to obtain permission to use the likeness of public figures that are deceased as well. The next case is an example of how even a drawing of the likeness of a deceased individual on merch can be problematic.

Comedy III Productions, Inc. (Plaintiff) v. Gary Saderup, Inc (Defendant) addresses lithographs and t-shirts containing images of the Three Stooges. Comedy III claimed that the lithographs and t-shirts printed by Gary Saderup infringed on its rights through the appropriation of their right of publicity of the deceased celebrities. Gary Saderup reproduced and sold charcoal drawings of the Three Stooges on lithograph prints and t-shirts without the consent of

Comedy III. As discussed previously, the right of publicity provides celebrities with a common law intellectual
property right in the economic value of their personae.
The person claiming to be violated has to have what is
called "standing." Meaning they have a right to pursue
a claim of wrongdoing against them. In California, the
right of publicity of a deceased individual is extended by
statute – California Code 9902 – to vest in the heirs and
assignees of deceased celebrities giving them standing.

Comedy III sued Gary Saderup, alleging a violation
of California Civil Code section 9902, seeking damages
and injunctive relief by preventing Gary Saderup from
selling the drawings or any other product with the Three
Stooges image or likeness. The California code states: "[a]
ny person who uses a deceased personality's name, voice,
signature, photograph, or likeness, in any manner… for
purposes of advertising or selling or soliciting purchases
of, products, merchandise, goods, or services, without
prior consent from the person or persons specified in
subdivision (c), shall be liable for any damages sustained
by the person or persons injured as a result…"

The court acknowledged that where to draw the
line between free expression and privacy rights is often
a difficult determination. In an attempt to resolve the
fundamental conflict between the First Amendment
and the right of publicity, the California Supreme Court

formulated a balancing test. The test looks at whether the work at issue includes significant creative elements, and if so, do the creative elements transform the work into more than a mere celebrity likeness or imitation. If there are significant creative details added to a reproduction of a celebrity image, the new work receives protection equal to that accorded to original works of art.

In viewing the products, the court could not identify significant transformative or creative contributions to the likeness of the Three Stooges. As a result, the court reasoned that if they were to decide the First Amendment protected Gary Saderup's depictions, they "could not perceive how the right of publicity would remain a viable right other than in cases of falsified celebrity endorsements." For that reason, the trial court entered judgment in favor of Comedy III and awarded damages of $75,000, an amount equal to the profits from the sale of the likeness of The Three Stooges, $150,000 in attorney's fees, and other costs asserted.

To protect the name, image, or likeness of a deceased individual, the individual's estate or assigned rights holder has to make sure the rights are secure on both a state and federal level. Every state does not operate like California by automatically protecting that right through a state statute. Some states require being proactive in claiming these rights as the rightful owner. If state law says that the right to publicity of a deceased person's image or likeness must be declared to protect it, the unauthorized user may not be liable for the use of the image or likeness if no one claims ownership. However, an unauthorized user could be liable for other infringements as discussed in the next case involving the unauthorized use of the likeness of the deceased

If you are a person who may have failed to secure rights in a deceased celebrity likeness, there may be other ways to prevail on a claim of unauthorized use. In the following case, let's look at what happens when a one Legal Code fails, but another prevails.

In *Fifty-Six Hope Road Music, Ltd. (Plaintiff) v. A.V.E.L.A. Inc.*, AND *Leo Valencia (Defendants)*, the plaintiff, Fifty-Six Hope Road Music, Ltd failed to follow state law requirements to protect its rights in the use of the image and likeness of musician Bob Marley.

According to the complaint filed in the case, Fifty-Six Hope Road Music is owned by Bob Marley's children. Over the years, the company has had to enforce its rights in the Bob Marley intellectual property by sending out approximately four hundred cease and desist letters and filing over twenty trademark, copyright, and right of publicity suits.

In this case, Fifty-Six initiated the action against A.V.E.L.A and Leo upon discovering t-shirts containing Marley's likeness on sale at Target. However, Fifty-Six failed to register a claim as successors in interest to Marley in compliance with Nevada law.

Nevada law states, "A successor in interest ... of a deceased person may file in the Office of the Secretary of State ... a verified application for registration of his or her claim. A successor in interest ... of a deceased person may not assert any right against any unauthorized commercial use of the deceased person's name, voice, signature, photograph or likeness that begins before the filing of an application to register his or her claim; State law requires a person claiming to be a successor in interest to a deceased person must, within six months after the date he becomes aware or should reasonably have become aware of unauthorized commercial use of the deceased person's name, voice, signature, photograph or likeness, register a claim with the Secretary of State pursuant to this subsection. Failure to register shall be deemed a waiver of any right of publicity."

Fifty-Six became aware of the unauthorized use of Marley's likeness when another person used his image before the alleged infringement by A.V.E.L.A, and Leo took place. Fifty-Six did not file a registration with the Secretary of State claiming its rights to a deceased celebrity figure within six months of the first alleged unauthorized use of Marley's likeness as required by state law. Therefore, Fifty-Six was unable to enforce rights related to Marley's intellectual property based on the right of publicity claim in this case for failing to adhere to the Legal Code.

Fortunately, Fifty-Six registered federal trademarks in the Bob Marley Brand. While Fifty-Six did not prevail on its right of publicity claim, the company did prevail on the trademark claim and was awarded $348,543.00 in profits and attorney fees from the defendants.

CONCLUSION

"I don't need to get my due; I get my money."
– Master P

A Fundamental Right

Using a person's image and likeness without permission is rampant in our society. Understandably, an aspect of communicating an idea is through the creation of visuals to support the message. However, problems arise when we are not conscious of what stands between the practice of the Street Code and prohibitions of the Legal Code. As discussed earlier, there are two distinct legal claims that the Legal Code allows individuals to assert for the unauthorized use of their identity. The first being invasion of privacy through misappropriation of name or likeness. The second is the violation of the right of publicity.

There are similarities and differences between misappropriation and right of publicity claims. Insight on how these rules apply in the state you operate in now or in the future will benefit you greatly. Learning this information can help protect your rights and prevent you from violating someone else's rights. Despite the slight variations in the two types of privacy protections, the intention of both is to protect a fundamental right: the right to privacy and protection from unauthorized use of one's likeness for a personal benefit to another, financially or otherwise.

Usually, people run into trouble when they use the name or photograph of an athlete, entertainer, or even those in the general public for commercial purposes such as in advertising or other promotional activities used to generate profit. However, there are times when people use someone's name or image for a business-related benefit that may not directly generate profit. You may think that what you are doing is not considered a commercial use if you don't earn money, but making a profit is not the only method a court will use to measure gain. Furthermore, some states prohibit the use of another person's identity for a personal benefit, whether the purpose is commercial or not.

Under the Legal Code, a person may possess several rights in one property. If you use something without authorization, you could find yourself charged with several violations for one use. Even if you can prove the right to use a person's property under one Legal Code, you could still be violating a right under another. We saw how this worked in favor of the plaintiff's Fifty-Six with the unauthorized use of Bob Marley's image. The defendants prevailed under the right of publicity claim but had to dish out a lot of money to Fifty-Six under the trademark claim.

The ability to be sued for different rights also means you could be liable to different rights holders. For example, recall the Lebron James case for copyright infringement discussed in the Copyright section of this guide? Although the photographer is the proper copyright owner of the photo, Lebron can enforce his rights regarding the image of him in the photo. Lebron retains the independent right to have his personality, name, image, and likeness —even if newsworthy— free from commercial exploitation at the hands of another. Therefore, he could assert privacy rights if his image in the photograph is used commercially without his permission. You recall Michael Jordan's case with the store advertisement. Under the right of publicity claim, Lebron could share in the profit obtained by the use of his likeness.

In summary, failure to obtain authorization for use can violate a variety of laws related to the right of publicity, trademarks, and copyrights.

Podcast and Social Media Problems

Podcasts and independent online media shows are popping up every day. The effects of the 2020 Covid-19 pandemic ushered in even more podcasts. Media is an area where people find themselves battling between the Street Code and the Legal Code. It is imperative to receive consent for the use of images, videos, sound recordings, and other media from the individual(s) appearing on a show. It is also imperative to only use that media for the purpose in which you received consent. Consent given to use a photograph does not permit you to use a recording for commercial purposes.

When taking photographs or video of someone, use a client release that covers both. When interviewing someone, issue an interview release that includes consent for the use of whatever you may need to promote your interview (photographs, voice recordings, etc.). If you are the person being interviewed, make sure you are clear on what you are giving consent for.

Secure Your Rights

Lastly, if you are the subject of a photograph, video, or sound recording, it is good practice to secure all your rights whenever possible.

As discussed in the Copyright section of this guide, you may be able to secure your rights if the photo, video, or sound recording is produced as a "work made for hire." For example, if an individual does a photoshoot, it may be helpful to enter into an express written agreement that the service is a "work made for hire" in which you retain all rights. "Work for hire" means the service is being specially ordered or commissioned for the type of work permitted under copyright law for such a claim. Remember, Nike argued that the "KL2" logo associated with Kawhi was a "work for hire." As a result, Nike retained owner-ship, although Kawhi was involved in the development process.

CODE V. CODE
CONTRACTS

Street Code v. Legal Code

United States (2020)

FACTS

---

*"Though no one can go back and make a brand-new start,
anyone can start from now and make a brand-new ending."*
- Carl Bard

The Anchor

The importance of understanding contracts touches all industries equally. Contract law is the anchor of all the topics discussed in this guide. The main reason for protecting your intellectual property is so you can capitalize on your creation or brand value. As discussed in the previous section, the use of your name, image, and likeness has value. If an individual would like to use your work, brand, or likeness, it is good practice to prepare a written document detailing the scope, conditions, and terms of use.

A contract is an agreement that creates an obligation based on promises. As you may know, a contract can be created verbally or in writing. However, where most people fall short in their understanding is that there are exceptions to this rule. Specific types of contracts must be in writing to be enforceable (more on this later). Whether an agreement is expressed in a written contract or verbally, if the necessary terms or conditions are missing or not communicated clearly, the agreement may not reflect your intentions and may not be enforceable. Therefore, it is important to understand what terms and conditions need to be acknowledged and agreed to by all parties.

Good Ol' Handshake

Contract law is the area most influenced by the Street Code. People ask, "What is wrong with a good ol' handshake?" Many athletes, entertainers, and entrepreneurs push back when advised to enter into legitimate contracts. Even if they agree to a written contract, many fail to read the document and do their due diligence to fully understanding the deals they enter into. Throughout my career, I have worked to resolve many disputes between parties in written contracts and verbal agreements. I have heard numerous reasons why the details of the agreement were not adequately documented. Here is a list of the top 5 reasons for not entering into written contracts that I have encountered:

1. The people agreeing to a promise are friends or family and feel it's not necessary to get so serious about entering into a contract.

2. The people agreeing to a promise think that the circumstances are not on a level to warrant a conversation about memorializing the contractual obligations

3. The people who are agreeing to the deal hate contracts.

4. Certain people agreeing to a promise felt intimidated by the others and were scared to ask to put the terms in writing because they thought it might mess up the opportunity.

5. One party to the deal is an athlete or entertainer who is not the least bit interested in handling the business side of the sports and entertainment industry.

This section of this empowerment guide will provide insight into the importance of a written contract, cultural conditioning supporting the Street Code mindset and the consequences of not having a documented agreement of understanding. Contract law is complicated. Therefore, it is good practice to hire a competent legal advisor who has your best interest in mind.

HISTORY

*"All of our experiences fuse into our personality.
Everything that ever happened to us is an ingredient."*
- **El-Hajj Malik El-Shabazz (Malcolm X)**

Broken Down

Each industry has its own background story and driving forces behind why contracts are viewed the way they are. This guide is aimed at empowering athletes, entertainers, and entrepreneurs to break out of the Street Code mindset and take control of their business lives and their future.

In my experience, the historical treatment and mental conditioning, or "cultural conditioning," in these industries has created a mindset of reluctancy to enter into contract negotiations, a timid demeanor during negotiations, or a complete "hand off" of contract dealings to someone else. This mindset creates an uneven playing field for athletes and entertainers who are generally not business-savvy and is widespread among minority athletes and entertainers.

Because I have experienced that this mindset is more prevalent in black athletes, I will discuss contracts in the sports industry and cultural conditioning from the perspective of the black athlete.

In the entertainment industry, the competitiveness to 'make it' entices many to agree to do things outside the contract, make promises, and agree to contract terms and conditions that are not in their best interest. Again, the cultural conditioning has influenced how black entertainers approach the business side of this industry. But unlike the sports industry, the entertainment industry is less forgiving across the board. Its discriminatory history has impacted how women, Latinos, Asian Americans, Native Americans, and the LGBTQ community handle the business side and approach contract dealings.

Entrepreneurs regularly rely on the Street Code when starting a small business and typically don't interact with an attorney in the beginning stages of establishing their business or at all. Not only does the Street Code impact an entrepreneur's decision-making regarding contract dealings, but cultural conditioning in all its forms can encourage bad business deals.

The Mindset and Sports

When we talk about sports and contract dealing, we are either speaking of the athlete or the individual or entity that they are in contract with. This guide aims at empowering the athletes; therefore, the discussion will spotlight the perspective and behavioral history of the athlete as a party to a contract.

To get full a grasp on the Street Code mindset driving the athlete and his or her beliefs about contracts, we need to go back to a time when athletes in the U.S. competed in sports for reasons other than to become professional athletes. To understand the journey of the black athlete, the conversation must go back in history during the time of slavery when sports had a different meaning.

During the time of enslavement, black athletes participated (most times involuntarily) in sports for the entertainment and money-making activities of slave owners. At times, enslaved people who participated in sport earned benefits that otherwise would not have been provided. If an athlete became dominant in their performance, they could "earn" freedom for them and/or their family or special status or privileges not extended to other enslaved black Americans. Doing well for their slave master meant they might have the opportunity to live in slightly better conditions than other enslaved individuals.

Frederick Douglass argued sports were a diversion tactic in the deep south to calm revolutionary inclinations of the enslaved sparked by anger and hostility. Individuals like Tom Molineaux boxed his way to freedom. William Mallory raced his way to bags of silver for his master. Charles Stewart trained horses and jockeyed his way to an elevated status. Whether the black athlete participated in sports to benefit a slave master, jockey to a higher status, box themselves to freedom, or influence a community of champions, there was one narrative stamped in the minds of all involved. The black athlete should be grateful for the opportunity even though it was an opportunity that they rightfully earned, and everyone benefitted from it. The experience of sport for such "freedoms" has had a lasting impression throughout the evolution of sports. This, unfortunately, is a lasting narrative that has infiltrated systems and continues to be embraced by a lot of black athletes.

Post emancipation, black athletes shifted their focus on using athleticism to attain power. Black athletes used their platforms to fight historical barriers and to be a force for change. There was little room for understanding or concentrating on negotiating the best contracts for their talent and skill. Participating in sports was a way of survival for the collective objectives of the black community. Even after slavery was abolished, sports were still being used as a method to transcend a system of inequality and gain "freedoms," freedom to vote, freedom of access, and economic freedom.

Fast forward many years later. Sports were used as an opening for black athletes to attend some of the most prestigious colleges in America. There was a sense of belonging and wanting to succeed in the big leagues that made certain opportunities attractive. Collegiate and professional sport was a chance to take part in what was considered the "big stage." Shiny promises seemed to shift a passion for influencing change to a desire to measure up. There were an eagerness and hope for the opportunity to "make it" in the black community. Families, coaches, and communities pushed athletes to sign any deal offered by those who could give athletes privileges that were generally unattainable or prohibited for blacks. The Street Code propagated the mindset, if you receive an offer from a college or a professional sports team, don't mess up or miss the opportunity. Because of the Street Code, athletes were encouraged to trust and accept whatever opportunity was offered. As a result, the mindset shifted from activism and advocacy to complacency.

This one-sided business interaction between the athlete and the individual, institution, corporation, or even the athlete's agent, created a mirroring of the enslavement era mindset. By failing to question the deal and create a contract in their own self-interest, the athlete allowed others to dictate their future. At no point in this process did black athletes become empowered to negotiate contracts with their best interests in mind.

My commentary is not to insinuate that non-black athletes have escaped the dog-eat-dog world of sports contracts. However, in my experience, the black athlete is negatively affected disproportionately by unfavorable contracts due to cultural conditioning. The disparaging impact has a lot to do with the mindset going into contract negotiations. Culturally, the black athlete is conditioned to go into these deals behind the eight ball.

SHOW-business

The entertainment industry is notorious for bad contracts. As with sports, I would be remiss not to note the black entertainer's cultural conditioning has also influenced contract dealings in the entertainment industry. In the entertainment industry, the competitiveness to 'make it' entices many to do things they usually wouldn't do, or accept things they normally wouldn't accept; to "compromise the soul" as it is called in the industry. This attitude is reflected in the actual contracts accepted and entered into. Entertainers are accustomed to focusing on the big word SHOW and little word business – "SHOWbusiness. In other words, the creative is more focused on the showing of creativity than understanding the business. The Street Code motto is to get your break now and worry about fully grasping the "devil in the details" or terms of the contract later.

There are many stories of artists and actors having their lives turned upside down over a contract. The next talent always believes the Street Code will work for them. They believe their situation, somehow, will be different.

If you are an entertainer or athlete reading this, I hope you are not going to bound to the Street Code. I anticipate you will take your business seriously and break the cultural beliefs that have shaped how and why contract deals have been one-sided.

Entrepreneur Seriousness

Too often, contractual agreements are entered into by an entrepreneur without the involvement of legal counsel or a competent level of understanding of contract formation. Whether the start-up provides a service or product, sometimes entrepreneurs fail to understand how many different contracts may apply to their business; employment, sales, and purchase contracts are all critical for a successful business. When it comes to entrepreneurs and contract dealing, there are so many moving parts to grasp that contract education should be a priority on the to-do-list. The common practice, however, is to get started, get things in order, and then, possibly, consider advice and counsel on drafting or entering into contracts. Too often, small business owners may think they have time to get serious about preventing legal issues later after the company is established.

Pick a well-known entrepreneur, and you may find that they experienced legal battles in their past from the lack of the business being legally sound, or they had to pay a hefty price tag to get out of a bad partnership. These entrepreneurs may be successful now, but they learned the hard way from their bad decisions and had to start all over to get it right. Getting it "right" commonly means, handling their business professionally throughout, from providing the service or product to making sure their paperwork is legitimate. Many start-up businesses and partnerships fail because the details of the relationship were not memorialized in writing. Instead, the entrepreneurs and partners relied on, and embraced, the handshake theory of the Street Code.

Cultural conditioning impacts the entrepreneur's decision-making process as well. The same history of dealings comes into play when the entrepreneur is a minority or is not business-minded. Minority business owners may be more apprehensive in asserting themselves in business deals or contract opportunities due to the experience of not being accepted or understood and may fear losing business if they do not agree with the deal before them.

If you are a start-up entrepreneur or small business owner, you may feel more comfortable operating under the Street Code. Still, you should understand that you have a vested interest in not cutting corners when it comes to contract dealings. It is up to you, the entrepreneur, to decide when and how you want to manage your business's legal decisions and related implications.

ISSUE

*"I just believe in ownership...
I believe in investing in yourself...
Your foundation should be strong."*
- **Nipsey Hussle**

Enforcing A Contract

Issues surrounding contract disputes are generally related to breach of performance and not having an enforceable agreement. Questions presented to me about contracts have been along the lines of the following:

1. "Can I enforce an agreement when we verbally agreed to the terms and conditions?" Sometimes people feel comfortable discussing business without putting the agreement in writing. They trust that each person will hold up to their part of the bargain.

2. "Can a contract be enforced if I did not understand the terms and conditions that I agreed to?" A lot of times, people do not read contracts thoroughly. They don't find out what they agreed to until an issue arises that brings attention to the contract terms.

3. "Is a contract that I found online good to use for my business if the terms are similar to the type of deal I'm negotiating?" People find templates on websites and use these templates rather than consult an attorney to save money.

4. "If I don't consider the deal a major opportunity, is a contract required?" A lot of times, people believe contracts only apply to certain types of opportunities or business relationships.

These are important questions that require thoughtful consideration. Understanding contract rules will help answer most of them. Seeing how courts have addressed some of these issues will also assist in shedding light on the consequences of taking short cuts.

RULES

"Only free men can negotiate,
prisoners can't enter in contracts."
- Nelson Mandela

Freedom to Contract

Contract law supports the free will to enter into an agreement. The law encourages the ability to exchange something of value for something more desirable to you with an expectation of fairness. The law also encourages individuals to predict the consequences of their actions. Because contract law stands on these premises, the courts do not like being asked to interfere with an agreement because they consider contracts between parties to be private dealings. It doesn't look good when the reason for soliciting the court's involvement is a result of disregarding the sound judgment of creating or reviewing the contract in the first place.

Enforceable Agreement

An agreement is enforceable when made under a valid contract. A valid written or oral contract will have the following elements: 1) offer, 2) acceptance, 3) mutual agreement, 4) consideration, 4) essential terms, and 5) legal capacity.

1. An offer is when someone makes an outward expression either in writing, orally, or through conduct. The intention of the offer suggests that acceptance will conclude the deal.

2. Acceptance must be communicated to the person that made the offer in a manner required by the person making the offer. Acceptance is generally conveyed in written or verbal form or, in some instances, communicating acceptance can be through silence when the offer states that silence is a form of approval. The form of acceptance is dictated by the terms required in the offer. If a person remained silent but took advantage of an offer when provided with a chance to reject it, silence could be a form of acceptance. If the circumstance or past dealings amongst the parties made it reasonable to believe an intention not to accept would have been communicated, silence could be a form of acceptance.

3. In establishing a mutual agreement among the parties to a contract, there must be an understanding that the "offeror" is making a present commitment to a legally binding offer, and acceptance of the offer will close the deal. The court will look at two things when deciding on whether there was

mutual consent to enter into a contract. First, was there an offer and acceptance. Second, can a reasonable person objectively look at the surrounding circumstances and conclude that there is an agreement.

4. Consideration is an exchange of promises or performance between the parties involved in the contract. In other words, a contract is a "this for that" exchange. Each person must receive something from the agreement; otherwise, the contract may not be enforceable and may be viewed as a gratuitous offer or a gift.

A contract is not valid unless the essential terms of the agreement are present. There is not a hard-set rule as to what terms need to be in a contract. However, there are bare minimum terms the courts consider essential and must be present. These terms are 1) quantity (any specific amount of an item), 2) identification of the parties (who is under the agreement), 3) price (any money exchanged), and 4) subject matter (the particular goods or service).

As touched on earlier, a contract does not have to be in writing. Contracts can be verbal. However, there are exceptions to enforcing oral contracts. Certain types of agreements are generally required to be in writing to make them enforceable. An agreement for marriage, sale of land, sale of goods greater than $500, assignment of an executor for the deceased, guarantee of debt, and long-term contracts performed for more than one year from the date of the agreement. These types of transactions are all on the exception list and are not enforceable if agreed to in an oral contract. Under the Legal Code, this list of exceptions is called the "Statute of Frauds." This guide will not go into too much detail about this list; just know there are exceptions to the oral contract rule. An exception to the oral contract rule of particular importance to athletes and entertainers are agreements that take longer than a year to fulfill. Contracts entered into by athletes and entertainers typically extend well beyond a year.

For entrepreneurs, it is imperative to be mindful of the exception for contracts for the sale of goods. Contracts for the sale of goods must be in writing if the total sale is over $500.

There are some defenses people can raise if they are unable to perform under a contract or that will allow them to get out of a contract without it being considered a breach. Each state has specific laws and language that may apply. In general, defenses to the enforceability of a contract are incapacity (minors), mental incompetence (not capable of understanding), misrepresentation (lies), duress (threat), undue influence (vulnerable), unconscionability (unreasonable bargaining process and terms), and public policy (illegal or violates certain rights and freedoms).

Incapacity is a defense often raised in sports and entertainment contract disputes as minors, generally individuals under the age of 18, are frequently parties to contracts in these industries. For those of you in the sports and entertainment industry that may work with minors, have a minor, or are a minor yourself, you should take special care with contract dealing.

APPLICATION

"Success does not consist in never making mistakes,
but in never making the same one a second time."
- **George Bernard Shaw**

Unconditional Ownership

Contracts memorialize the intent of a business deal or a simple agreement. Although the Street Code may label contracts as something to cringe at or avoid at all costs if possible, they are necessary and only take on the tenor of "evil" if one fails to understand what is being agreed to. As the saying goes, "the devil is in the details." The details are what all parties to an agreement should familiarize themselves with. If you are the one negotiating, or you hire someone to do so on your behalf, reading the terms and conditions in the contract thoroughly can eliminate or reduce the headaches and heartaches.

Demanding that a contract "seal the deal" does not mean that there is a lack of trust, and it doesn't mean the contract has to be complicated or complex. What a contract should indicate is that each person wants to communicate an agreement in a mutually beneficial way to perform or not perform an action, or to provide or not provide a product, for some form of consideration. It is best to put any agreement down on paper so that all parties are clear on the expectations. Putting the agreement in writing keeps communication intact and allows for an easy reference if anyone happens to forget the terms and conditions of the agreement.

Contract issues are problematic in the sports and entertainment industry. Often problems arise with artists in record deals and athletes in sports deals. For the reasons discussed in the History section, the Street Code encourages the mindset to enjoy now and think later. The belief is that the essential term to a contract is the one that has a dollar sign. You should know that the key details surrounding those financial terms need to be reviewed carefully. In the sports and entertainment industries, you are either owned, owning, or collaborating. The person who signs documents without understanding the details is usually the one who ends up being owned by the industry. Empower yourself to come to the table with the knowledge to walk away with ownership or collaboration.

The following cases will put this information into perspective when you see how issues arise from the Street Code's influence when navigating in these industries.

Ronnie Greenfield (Plaintiff and Respondents) v. Philles Records, Inc (Defendant and Appellants) is a typical case of what can happen when someone does not review a contract thoroughly or at all. In the early 1960s, two sisters and their cousin formed a singing group. They signed a two-page contract with a record production company. The group executed the agreement without the benefit of counsel. The members of the group agreed to perform exclusively for Philles Records. According to the agreement, the company acquired ownership rights to the group's recordings and agreed to pay royalties.

The group disbanded, and the production company continued to sell albums containing the group's songs. The production company also licensed the master recordings for use in movies and television productions. In this suit alleging breach of contract, the state high court held that the signed agreement gave the record production company unconditional ownership rights to the group's master recording. The contract only required payment of royalties to members of the group.

The court expressed that it enforces an agreement based on the parties' intent. The best evidence is to look at a written agreement to see what the parties intend by what they say in their writing. Thus, a written contract that is complete, clear, and unambiguous is enforceable according to the plain meaning of its terms. According to the terms, the royalty schedule was for domestic sales. The group was not entitled to profits earned off the license of the performances for use in visual media such as movies, television commercials, or broadcasts. Nor was the group allowed to benefit from the domestic release of its music by third parties in audio formats.

The court stated that it realized the decision it will impose would effectively prevent the plaintiffs from sharing in the profits the defendants received from synchronization licensing. However sympathetic it was to the plaintiffs' plight, the court could not resolve the case on that ground. The court noted it "must decide under the canons of contract construction. The guiding principle must be to apply the rules of contract interpretation neutrally. Only in this way can the court ensure stability in the law and guide parties weighing the risks and advantages of entering a binding agreement." Judgment was in favor of Philles Records.

The court made it clear that the written contract is the best evidence of people's intentions. This is why it is important to know what is written in a contract. If your intentions are anything contrary to a document you sign, a court may be sympathetic to your outcome, but not influenced by it. Unless a legal defense applies to the situation, you will be stuck with what you agreed to. Even if that means you agreed to lose it all.

Fail Under Copyright Prevail Under Contract

It is a good idea to secure and exercise as much protection afforded to a proprietary right as you can. You can protect property interests in more than one way. Doing so will give you more than one fight. The Legal Code, in this respect, extends various options to ensure the protection of creative works. Creating different avenues to protect intellectual and personal property encourages and fosters a fundamental respect for individual development and self-realization.

For example, an implied contract can offer protection when copyright protection is not enough. In *Victor Desny, (Plaintiff and Appellant) v. Billy Wilder, Paramount Pictures Corporation (Defendants and Respondents),* a breach of contract claim prevailed when copyright protection failed.

In this case, Victor filed a claim for story theft. He shared his story with Billy's secretary so that she could give it to Billy (he was her boss) for consideration. In writing, Victor communicated to the secretary his expectation of payment if they used the story, ideas, themes, or information contained in the story with or without his permission. Victor later discovered that Paramount made a movie based on the story presented to Billy. The court sided with Victor's argument of story theft because his written communication with the secretary created an implied contract. He put in writing what his expectations were if anyone used the story. The secretary agreed to the terms by accepting the information. The court concluded that Billy produced his version based on Victor's idea because it included a fictionalized incident that Victor created in his script. Victor won his story theft claim under an implied contract theory. He would not have prevailed under copyright because what he shared was considered an idea that could not be protected by copyright law.

If you recall in the Copyright section, I listed what can and cannot be protected by copyright law. An idea is something that cannot be protected if it is not expressed or expressed in a way that makes is creative. A court may look at the sharing of a story as an idea like it did in this case, and not necessarily a creative expression of authorship (which is protected). Since you don't know how a court may analyze your situation, you should avail yourself of all protections that apply to a business transaction. In this case, Victor's claim of copyright infringement was a fail, but his argument of breach of contract allowed him to prevail against the "story thieves." Be a 'Victor' in your situation.

If your script is protected under copyright law, unlike Victor's, a court can still find that certain elements are not protected, and therefore, can be copied by others. Remember the Metcalfs case discussed earlier in the Copyright section of this guide? In that case, the Metcalfs, the court considered their script more than a mere idea. Their script was an expression of authorship protected under copyright. Even with copyright protection, the Metcalfs had to pass the "substantially similarities test" assessed by courts to prevail in their copyright lawsuit. Under this test, the court compared elements of their copyrightable work to the defendant's work. If the copyrighted elements weren't enough to succeed on the infringement claim, they would have failed the test. An implied contract could have been a second argument for them. The implied contract argument would have only applied if the Metcalfs handled the sharing of their script under the protection of contract law.

Let me share another case with you to give an example of a story theft where the plaintiffs presented both legal arguments to the court and how the court addressed these issues.

In, *Aaron Benay and Matthew Benay (Plaintiffs-Appellant) v. Warner Bros. Entm't Inc. et al., (Defendants-Appellees),* Aaron and Matthew argued copyright protection and breach of implied contract for story theft.

Aaron and Matthew wrote and copyrighted a screenplay titled "The Last Samurai." They alleged that the creators of the film, also titled "The Last Samurai," copied from the screenplay without permission. They filed for copyright infringement under federal law and breach of contract under California law.

Aaron and Matthew sued Warner Brothers Entertainment, Inc., Radar Pictures, Inc., Bedford Falls Productions, Inc., Edward Zwick, Marshall Herskovitz, and John Logan, all of whom wrote, produced, marketed, and/or distributed the film. Under the copyright claim, the court analyzed the two works to determine if the copyright-protected elements were substantially similar. The court ruled in favor of the defendants concluding that the screenplay and the film were not substantially similar for purposes of copyright infringement.

The copyright infringement ruling did not preclude the court analysis for story theft under an implied-in-fact contract. Under California law, the court laid out the case for breach of an implied-in-fact contract which required Aaron and Matthew to establish six factors to support enforcement of the contract:

1. they submitted the screenplay for sale to the defendants;
2. they conditioned the use of the screenplay on payment;
3. the defendants knew or should have known of the conditions;
4. the defendants voluntarily accepted the screenplay;
5. the defendants used the screenplay; and
6. the screenplay had value.

The court remarked, to preserve the state cause of action, the court must address the protection of rights that are qualitatively different from the rights protected by copyright. The state's cause of action must allege an "extra element" that changes the nature of the federal copyright action. The court ruled the "extra element" in this case was the bilateral expectation of compensation; both parties expected to be compensated by the work. Therefore, the court accepted Aaron's and Matthew's claim based on contract law. Proving substantial similarity of copyright-protected elements was not necessary.

So again, taking all protective measures available increases protections and chances of triumph in a court of law.

Major in Minors

As mentioned in the Rules section above, incapacity is one of the defenses for breach of contract. The general rule is that contractual agreements with minors (look to state law for appropriate age) are voidable. There is a special consideration that applies to minors in sports and entertainment. Hence, there are specific factors to consider when working with minors in these industries. As with other laws, each state has its Legal Code to regulate the making of contracts with minors. Federal law doesn't interfere (unless they have to) with state regulation regarding these relationships other than providing an exception to the Fair Labor Standard Act. This exception is for child entertainers employed as actors or performers in motion pictures, theatrical productions, or radio and television productions.

Children are a source of considerable revenue. They have made tremendous contributions to the overall success of film, television, and music. Most state laws attempt to balance a need to uphold the validity of a contract on the one end and to provide protection for child actors on the other.

California, New York, and Florida are three states that employ a lot of child actors. These states have legislation in place requiring contracts with minors to be approved by the court. But even in these states, adherence to these statutes is still at the discretion of the producer or manager.

With Georgia growing in the film industry, we probably can expect to see some changes in legislation protecting child entertainers. GA. Code 13-3-21 states, "If a minor, by permission of his parent or guardian or by permission of law, practices any profession or trade or engages in any business as an adult, he shall be bound for all contracts connected with such profession, trade, or business." As of now, with the current law, Georgia does not have legislation requiring court approval of contracts with minors. Many of the contracts made with minors in the industry today are not court-approved, yet, the contracts are still valid.

Representatives of child performers should exercise the Legal Codes available to their fullest extent if doing so would be in the best interest of the child. Although circumventing court approval will not render the contract itself void, failure to get court approval, if required, can backfire on the individual or entity employing the child. This is something to consider if you are the one employing a minor, and you operate under the Street Code of court evasion. I will share a case in this section on what could happen if you live in a state that encourages seeking court approval for contracts with minors, and you don't.

The Street Code's behavior of wheeling and dealing with minors results in broken promises, vulnerable children who may be injured, and putting lots of money at risk. The Street Code encourages the mindset to "get the most out of kids now." When it is all said and done, it is in the courtroom where the final act plays out, and the saddest songs are sung.

In *Bright Tunes, Productions, Inc. (Plaintiff) v. Barbara Lee, et al.* (Defendants), Bright Tunes sought to enforce a contract that was not approved by the court at any time before or during the contract's term. Bright Tunes tried to prevent the defendants from performing or rendering any services as recording artists for anyone other than Bright Tunes during the term of the contract. In the lawsuit, Bright Tunes demanded damages for breach of contract.

Bright Tunes entered into a written agreement with Barbara and the other defendants. They engaged the girls to render exclusive personal service as recording artists for the production of phonograph records. The term was for one year and granted Bright Tunes four one-year options to renew the agreement. The options ran consecutively for a total duration if exercised of five years. Upon the execution of the original contract, the parents warranted to Bright Tunes that each defendant was over the age of 18 years old and, therefore, were not minors. However, none of the defendants was then over the age of 18 except Barbara. The girls were all over the age of 18 at the time they wanted to disaffirm the contract.

The court did not approve the contract in question before the close of the deal as approval was not required. Nonetheless, the court looked at the intent of the legislature as applied to court approval for contracts with minors. In doing so, it recited, "No contract shall be approved if its terms, including any extensions thereof by option or otherwise, extend for a period of more than three years from the date of approval of the contract. Or if it contains any covenant or condition binding upon the infant beyond such three years. Such contracts, under the circumstances, would not be reasonable and provident."

After reviewing the facts of the case, the court reasoned "a contract hereafter made by an infant after he has attained the age of eighteen years may not be disaffirmed by him on the ground of infancy, where the contract was made in connection with a business in which the infant was engaged and was reasonable and provident when made." In layman's terms, the court was saying a contract with a minor may not be canceled because of age if the purpose for the contract is for business and the terms of the agreement were reasonable and considerate of how the conditions could impact the minor in the future.

Because the contract in the Bright Tunes case was with minors, and the term extended for more than three years, the court held that the contract with the girls, infants now over 18 years of age, was as a matter of law, unreasonable and improvident. Therefore, the defendants had a right to disaffirm the contract in question. Had the contract called for a shorter term of two or three years, the defendants may not have prevailed.

Now let's go back to the point made earlier about operating under the Street Code of circumventing court approval for a contract with a minor. If Bright Tunes had followed the Legal Code, the renewal option in the contract could have been identified as problematic by the reviewing court opinions. Early detection would have allowed them to fix the term to reflect three years, which was more considerate of the girls' future according to the law and may have allowed Bright Tunes to prevail on the breach of contract claim.

CONCLUSION

"Start where you are. Use what you have. Do what you can."
- ***Arthur Ashe***

Where You See Yourself

Failure to gain an understanding of your rights and responsibilities under contract law can leave you legally, practically, and often financially vulnerable. In viewing contract terms, consider where you are now and where you see yourself going. It may be necessary to revisit and amend contract terms over time as your career grows.

In looking at Kawhi's situation in the Copyright section, an amendment to the terms in his contract could have resulted in a different outcome in his fight to maintain ownership of his logo. A simple revision to address the work for hire language in his initial contract to later exclude his logo may have resolved any future issues. Even if the court held the logo as being transformative, if Kawhi had a written agreement that any variations of the logo would rightfully be his, the logo would still be his today. If he had registered copyright for the logo, he might have succeeded in defending his ownership of the logo under the Legal Code that way. I'm sure the relationship was great in the beginning, and there was trust there. But business is business. The terms Kawhi initially agreed to with Nike were not beneficial to him after their breakup when the relations went sour. Operating under the Street Code made it too late for him to fight.

In addition to securing any federal protection that may be available for intellectual property, it may be helpful to consider other layers of protection available for a single piece of work. A contract can complete a full circle of security in your business dealing. If a court finds an issue with a copyright infringement claim because the elements in question are not protectable under copyright, a contract could be the next best safeguard. If an issue with a trademark infringement case fails because the court considers the mark descriptive in nature and a secondary meaning has not been established with consumers (which will invalidate it), a contract can catch the fall.

Even if someone has the best intentions, a breakdown in communication is not unforeseeable. Putting everything down on paper encourages everyone to examine each other's specific expectations. A contract is a document that can be pulled out later in case someone needs to refresh their memory on the terms or conditions of the agreement during the course of dealing. Relying on a verbal agreement can be just as shaky as a person's memory, and as previously discussed, there are exceptions to the enforceability of oral contracts. Contracts are not bad.

However, not properly reviewing or understanding the terms of a contract is.

KEY TAKEAWAY

If you are going to expect change, it must start with you. What you expect from others you have to expect from yourself. Without athletes, entertainers, or entrepreneurs, there wouldn't be thriving industries that create so much business for people to get rich off. What side to the tracks will you find yourself on in these multi-billion and trillion-dollar industries? The answer to this depends on the initiative you take to empower yourself on the matters that affect sustainable economic inclusion and real ownership. From my experience and study, the common issue with the four areas that present an imbalance with parties to a business deal is the lack of possessing the necessary knowledge in the areas Copyright, Trademark, Right to Privacy, and Contracts.

Operating under the Street Code may provide short term benefits, and you may witness these temporary gains by watching others and measure it as some sort of success. However, If you want to be competitive and maximize your leverage, you must operate under the Legal Code applicable in that situation at the time. If you don't like the Legal Code, fight to change it. Don't put yourself in a position where you could lose everything by repeating a cycle, or from not understanding how to be the CEO of your brand. You are the gatekeeper of your talents and gifts.

As noted in the introduction, this empowerment guide is for any athlete, entertainer, or entrepreneur who is currently in these industries or looking to be. Also, as I acknowledged in my writing, some individuals experience being vulnerable or targeted in these industries because of gender, sexuality, race, lack of resources, or other factors. However, the inspiration behind my words comes from a place of passion for encouraging the black community to know and do better. There is a need to realize ourselves as the athlete and the owner; the entertainer and the major entertainment company; the consumer buying "high-end brands" and the supplier selling high-end brands. Being the latter will outlive the former. Unfortunately, there is a disproportionate representation of black individuals when looking at both sides of this spectrum. I believe the first step to making a shift is in understanding how to transcend cultural conditioning.

To all of the readers, I implore you to use this guide, which has presented content, context, and cases as a nudge in letting the Legal Code lead your thoughts and actions to prevent harming others and being harmed by others.

SUMMARY OF RESOURCES

The information in the following section includes the significant sources used for the material contained in this empowerment guide. This summary is not all-inclusive, as it does not include every source researched or studied over the years of my legal profession. Nor does it encompass the vast majority of documents, client privileged information, work product, or other data and ideas I've gathered over the years working in these industries as an athlete, entrepreneur, or attorney. I attempted to include the most significant sources of information in this book that would help assist the reader in investigating the information shared and encourage further learning on the subjects discussed.

Part I – Copyright

WWW.COPYRIGHT.GOV

https://www.copyright.gov/fair-use/

https://www.copyright.gov/title17/

Copyright Act, 17 U.S.C, § 107-122

Hip-Hip Evolution, Shad Kabango, streaming documentary, Netflix

Katie Perry did not rip off "Dark Horse" from Christian rap song, judge rules. https://www.cbsnews.com/news/katy-perry-did-not-rip-off-dark-horse-from-christian-rap-song-judge-rules/

Complaint (Jury Trial Demanded) Steven Mitchell v. Lebron James, Uninterrupted Digital Ventures, LLC and LRMR Ventures, LLC., No. 1:20-cv-2374, UNITED STATES

Kawhi Leonard, v. Nike Inc., Case No. 3:19-cv-01586-MO, UNITED STATES DISTRICT COURT FOR THE DISTRICT OF OREGON; Kawhi Leonard v. NIKE INC. (D. Or. 2020) DISTRICT COURT SOUTHERN DISTRICT OF NEW YORK

Austris Wihtol v. Nelson E. Crow, 309 F.2d 777 (8th Cir. 1963)

Brownmark Films, LLC v. Comedy Partners and MTV Networks, 40 Media L. Rep. 1077, 100 U.S.P.Q.2d 1844, 800 F.Supp.2d 991, 2011 Copr.L.Dec. P 30106 (E.D. Wis. 2011)

Entertainment, Inc., a corporation; and Michael Warren, 294 F.3d 1069 (9th Cir. 2002)

Grand Upright Music v. Warner Bros. Records, Inc., 780 F. Supp. 182 (S.D. N.Y. 1991)

Gross et al. v. Seligman et al., 212 F. 930 (2ⁿᵈ Cir. 1914)

Jerome C. Metcalf and Laurie Metcalf v. Bochco Steven Productions, a corporation; CBS Entertainment, Inc., a corporation; CBS Productions, Inc., a corporation; Michael L. Warren, an individual; Nicholas Wootton, an individual; Paris Barclay, an individual, 294 F.3d 1069 (9th Cir. 2002)

Lebbeus Woods v. Universal City Studios, Inc., 920 F.Supp. 62 (S.D. N.Y. 1996)

Marcus Gray et al. v. Katheryn Hudson et al., 9th Cir. App. (2019)*; (see appeal) GRAY; ET AL. V. PERRY; ET AL.,* 2:15-CV-05642-CAS-JCx, March 16, 2020

Russell Brammer v. Violent Hues Productions, LLC., 922 F.3d 255 (4th Cir. 2019)

Stephanie Lenz v. Universal Music Corp., 801 F.3d 1126, 115 U.S.P.Q.2d 1965 (9th Cir. 2015)

Part II – Trademark
WWW.USPTO.GOV

Lanham Act, 15 U.S.C. § 1051 - U.S. Code

Abercrombie & Fitch Co. v. Hunting World, Inc., (2nd Circuit, 1976)

B. Leidersdorf v. J.G. Flint (1878), Circuit Court, Eastern District of Wisconsin

Brother Records, Inc. v. Jardine, 318 F.3d 900 (9th Cir. 2003)

Dallas Cowboys Cheerleaders Inc. v. Pussycat Cinema Ltd., 604 F.2d 200, 203 USPQ 161 (2nd Cir. 1979)

Fifty-Six Hope Road Music, Ltd. v. A.V.E.L.A. Inc., 688 F. Supp.2d 1148 (D. Nev. 2010)

Fleischmann Distilling Corp. (Plaintiff) v. Maier Brewing Co., (Defendant) (9th Circuit, 1963)

Gerald. Caiafa, Robert C. Kaufhold and Joseph Arthur McGukin v. Cyclopian Music, INC. et al., 872 F.Supp.2d 374 (D. N.J. 2012)

Timelines, Inc. v. Facebook, Inc., 938 F.Supp.2d 781 (N.D. Ill. 2013)

UNDERSTANDING MICHAEL JORDAN v. QIAODAN: HISTORICAL ANOMALY OR SYSTEMIC FAILURE TO PROTECT CHINESE CONSUMERS?, Laura Wen-yu Young Vol. 106 Trademark Reporter

Part III – Right of Publicity

The Right to Privacy, 4 Harvard L.R. 193 (1890)

Charles Ainsworth v. Century Supply Co., 295 Ill. App. 3d 644, 230 Ill. Dec. 381, 693 N.E.2d 510 (1998)

Comedy III Productions, Inc. v. Gary Saderup, Inc., 25 Cal.4th 387, 106 Cal.Rptr.2d 126, 21 P.3d 797 (Cal. 2001)

Fifty-Six Hope Road Music, Ltd. v. A.V.E.L.A. Inc., Leo Valencia, 778 F.3d 1059 (9th Cir. 2015)

Haelan Laboratories, Inc. v. Topps Chewing Gum, Inc., 202 F.2d 866 (2d Cir. 1953)

Lindsay Bullard (Plaintiff) v. Joe Francis and MRA Holding, LLC (Defendant), 292 Ga. 748, 740 S.E.2d 622 (Ga. 2013)

Michael Jordan v. Jewel Food Stores, Inc., 83 F.Supp.3d 761, 113 U.S.P.Q.2d 2093 (N.D. Ill. 2015)

Paolo Pavesich v. New England Life Insurance Co., 122 Ga. 190, 50 S.E. 68 (Ga. 1905)

People for the Ethical Treatment of Animals (PETA (Apellants)) v. Bobby Bersoni (Respondent), 895 P.2d 1269 (Nev.,1995)

Veronica Lane (Plaintiff) v. MRA Holdings, LLC. (Defendant), 242 F. Supp. 2d 1205 (M.D. Fla. 2002)

Part IV – Contracts

Fair Labor Standards Act of 1938 29 U.S.C. § 203

Forty Million Dollar Slaves: The Rise, Fall, and Redemption of the Black Athlete, William C. Rhodes

Minors -- Contracts relating to practice of profession, trade, or business *O.C.G.A. § 13-3-21 (2010).*

Aaron BENAY; Matthew Benay, individually, (Plaintiffs-Appellant) v. Warner BROS. Entertaintment, Inc., a Delaware corporation; et al. (Defendants-Appellees), 607 F.3d 620 (9th Cir. 2010)

Bright Tunes Productions, Inc. v. Lee, 249 N.Y.S.2d 632, 43 Misc.2d 21 (N.Y. Sup. Ct. 1964)

Act

Ronnie Greenfield v. Philles Records, Inc., 98 N.Y.2d 562, 750 N.Y.S.2d 565, 780 N.E.2d 166 (N.Y. 2002)

Victor Desny, (Plaintiff and Appellant) v. Billy Wilder, Paramount Pictures Corporation (Defendants and Respondents), 286 P.2d 55 (Cal. App. 1955)

www.ingramcontent.com/pod-product-compliance
Lightning Source LLC
Chambersburg PA
CBHW070040100426
42740CB00013B/2737